GUIDELINES FOR PREPARING AND USING A DESIGN AND MONITORING FRAMEWORK

SOVEREIGN OPERATIONS AND TECHNICAL ASSISTANCE

DECEMBER 2024

These guidelines describe how a project-level design and monitoring framework (DMF) should be developed and used throughout the
project cycle for sovereign operations and technical assistance. The DMF is a key tool for project design, implementation, and evaluation,
and provides the basis for the project performance management system of the Asian Development Bank (ADB). These guidelines are a
resource to assist staff of ADB, government officers, consultants, project sponsors and borrowers, and other stakeholders in preparing
a high-quality DMF and using it effectively as a tool to ensure ADB-financed projects contribute to the prosperous, inclusive, resilient,
and sustainable Asia and Pacific region envisaged by ADB's Strategy 2030. The guidelines are updated from time to time. While the
guidelines offer helpful information, adherence to them remains recommended but not mandatory, except those aspects made certain
and compulsory by existing policies.

CONTENTS

TABLES, FIGURES, AND BOXES

TABLES

FIGURES

BOXES

ABBREVIATIONS

ADB	Asian Development Bank
CPS	country partnership strategy
CSO	civil society organization
DMC	developing member country
DMF	design and monitoring framework
km	kilometer
M&E	monitoring and evaluation
NA	not applicable
PAM	project administration manual
PCR	project completion report
RAMP	risk assessment and risk management plan
RRP	report and recommendation of the President
TA	technical assistance
ToC	theory of change
TVET	technical and vocational education and training

THE DESIGN AND MONITORING FRAMEWORK: A TOOL FOR MANAGING FOR DEVELOPMENT RESULTS

These guidelines describe how the design and monitoring framework (DMF) should be developed and used throughout the project cycle for sovereign operations and technical assistance (TA). The DMF is the main tool that the Asian Development Bank (ADB) uses for managing for development results at the project level, and a core element of ADB's project performance management system.[1]

Managing for development results is a management approach that supports better performance and greater accountability by applying a clear, logical framework to plan, measure, and manage a project with a focus on the intended development results. It is a process of continuously learning and taking evidence-based decisions to improve performance. By clearly identifying the intended results of a project in advance, regularly collecting information to assess progress toward them, and taking timely corrective action, the project team is better able to maximize achievement of sustainable development results for ADB's developing member countries (DMCs).

Formulating a quality DMF is an essential first step in the project management cycle. In this process, a project team must understand the stakeholders and their problems and develop possible solutions into a manageable initiative. The basic steps in the project management cycle are as follows:

(i) identify results (outputs and outcome) and the causal relationships between them;
(ii) identify alignment with the broader sector- or country-level results (impact);
(iii) identify the external factors that could influence success or cause failure (risks and critical assumptions);
(iv) select indicators to measure performance, identify baselines, and decide on targets to be achieved;
(v) implement activities to deliver outputs;
(vi) measure and analyze data, and use them to assess project performance (monitoring and evaluation [M&E]);
(vii) report on results achievement and make project management decisions based on evidence of performance; and
(viii) learn about success and failure and integrate the lessons back into the project cycle.

The DMF-related milestones are shown in **Figure 1**.

Preparing the design and monitoring framework (Sections II and III). As the basic source of information about planned performance, the DMF plays a central role in ADB's project management cycle. All DMFs should be formulated through a participatory process (**Section III**) and reflect an approach and format suitable to a modality or product type. A preliminary DMF is included in project concept notes. Although the level of detail that the preliminary DMF contains will vary depending on how far the project planning has progressed, it includes at least an indicative impact statement and results chain, and general ideas for performance indicators. The target and baseline values for these indicators may not yet be determined. The DMF is further developed and agreed upon with key stakeholders during the fact-finding stage, and the confirmed DMF is attached to approval documents such as reports and recommendations of the President (RRPs).

Using the design and monitoring framework during project implementation. Facilitated by the project's M&E arrangements (**Section IV.A**), progress on DMF performance indicators is tracked and reported regularly, at least once a year, as part of project performance reporting.

---

[1] Unless otherwise stated, the term project is used throughout these guidelines as a general reference to cover all types of ADB sovereign investment products and TA.

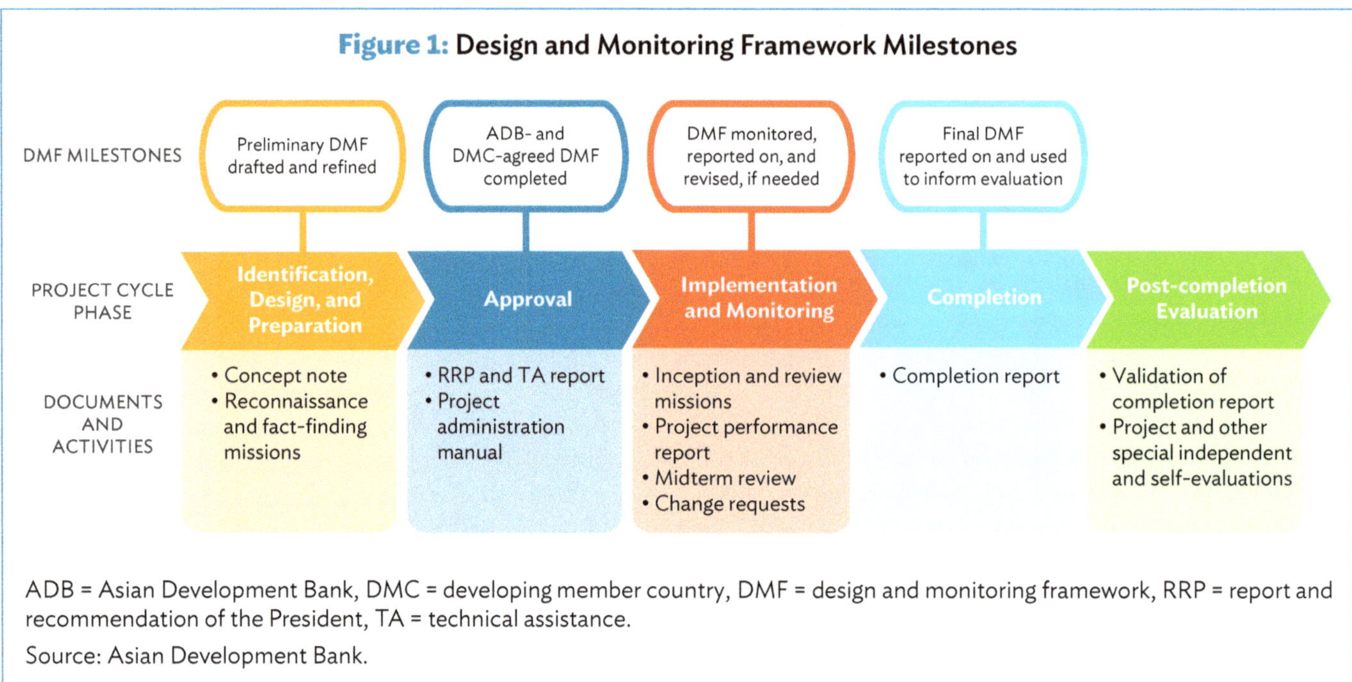

Figure 1: Design and Monitoring Framework Milestones

ADB = Asian Development Bank, DMC = developing member country, DMF = design and monitoring framework, RRP = report and recommendation of the President, TA = technical assistance.

Source: Asian Development Bank.

The DMF is updated throughout the project cycle to reflect all pertinent changes to the project following the procedures in the project administration instructions.[2] If the project scope changes, the degree to which the DMF must be changed determines the approval authority required (**Section IV.B**).

Using the design and monitoring framework after project completion. The DMF forms the basis of the completion reports for all projects, and project success is evaluated and rated against the DMF results chain and performance indicators (**Section IV.C**).

II DESIGN AND MONITORING FRAMEWORK STRUCTURE

The DMF captures critical information about the project in a matrix (Figure 2). The top row of the DMF may contain a maximum of three impact statements with which the project is aligned. For sovereign projects, these statements are typically derived from a regional, national, subnational, or sector plan or strategy. The matrix contains:

(i) the results chain, including the inputs, or main resources; the activities or groups of tasks; the outputs delivered by the project; and the outcome it will achieve;
(ii) performance indicators for measuring results achievement, targets to be achieved, and a baseline of current performance;
(iii) data sources and reporting mechanisms for each indicator; and
(iv) the risks that act against results achievement, and critical assumptions that underlie the results chain.

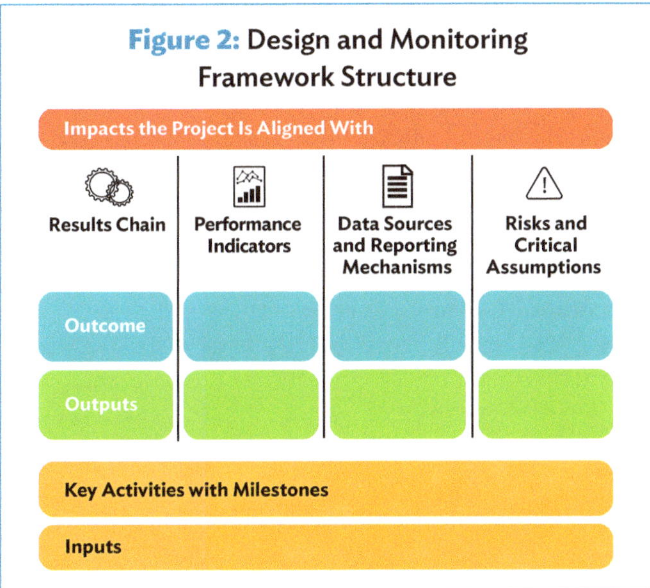

A. Results Chain

The primary purpose of a project is to achieve results that meet people's and/or organizations' needs. A results chain consists of a series of expected achievements, or positive changes, linked by causality. The results chain is a continuum from inputs to activities to outputs, and to outcomes. Outputs are defined as goods, products, or services delivered by the project, while outcomes are the immediate and direct benefits of the use or application of the outputs. The following are important pointers for developing a results chain:

(i) The alignment points for a project's results chain are impact statements, which are typically higher-level regional, national, subnational, or sector results to which the project contributes. The impact statement aligns the project's outcome with a higher-level development result.
(ii) The basic definitions and impact alignment are illustrated in Figure 3 using the example of an urban rail transit system project. The project delivers the following outputs: signaling, train control, and telecommunications systems operational; rolling stock operational; and institutional capacity of metro operations organizations strengthened. The outcome or the immediate and direct benefit for residents of City A, the ultimate intended beneficiary group, is that the efficiency, safety, and gender- and social-inclusiveness of the rail-based urban transit system in City A is enhanced. This outcome is aligned with the higher-level impact, i.e., "connectivity for all to social and economic opportunities in City A is improved."
(iii) The importance of the results increases moving up the results chain: efficient, safe, and inclusive transit is more important than an operational metro system, which is just a means to that end; and connectivity for all to social and economic opportunities is even more important. However, project control and accountability decreases moving up the results chain.

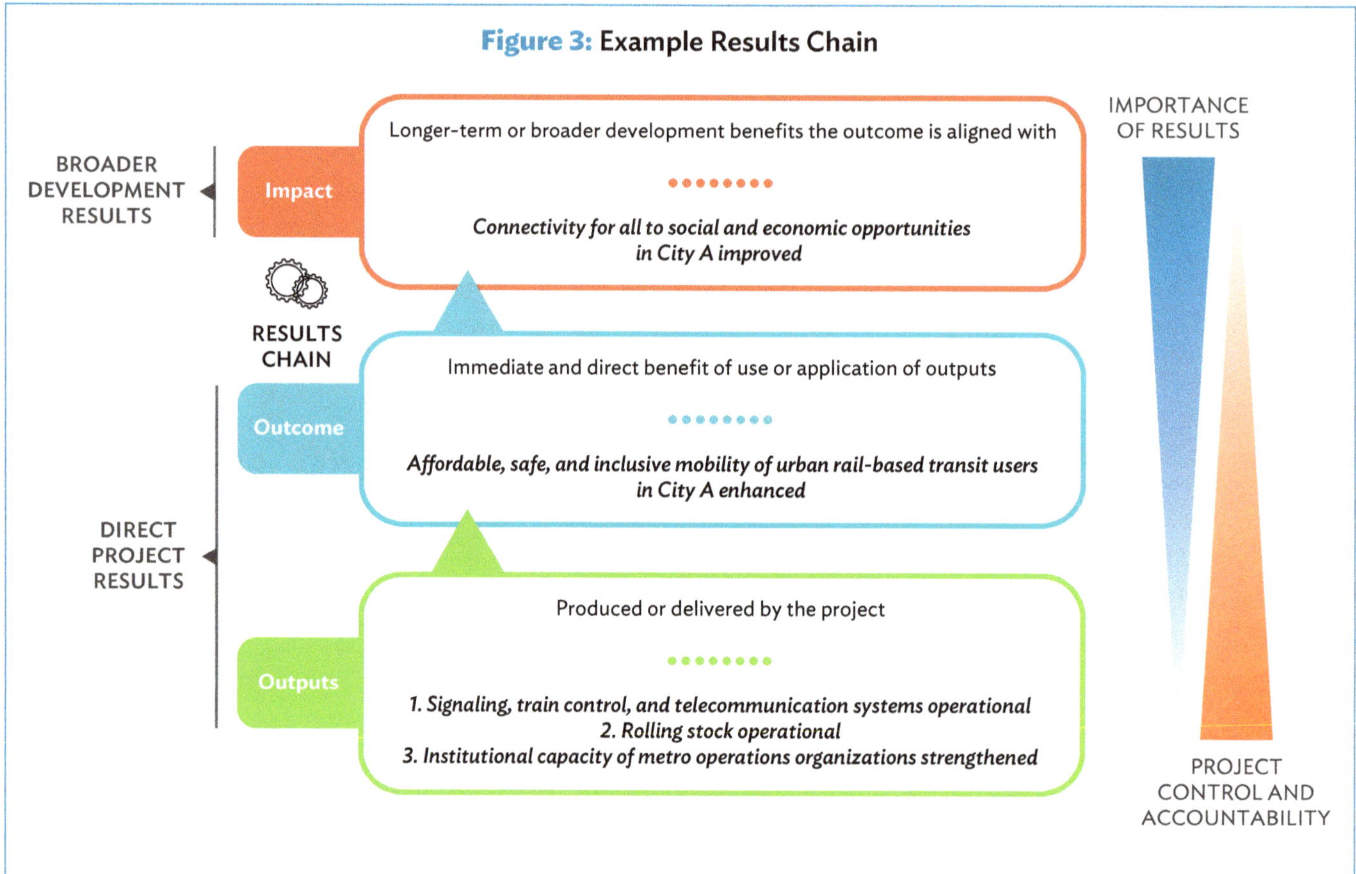

Figure 3: Example Results Chain

The project controls railway construction and capacity building, but it only influences the efficiency, safety, and inclusiveness of the rail-based urban transit system. The project is accountable for output delivery and outcome achievement, but not for impact-level results. Attribution also decreases from output and outcome to impact. The outputs and outcome are attributable to the project but the impact statement of "increased income for the industrial labor force" is outside the project results chain and, although the project contributes to it to some degree, it is not controlled by or attributed to the project.

Table 1 illustrates the differences among the results levels. It contains several concepts, including targets and assumptions for partner financing, which are discussed in subsequent sections of these guidelines.

Outputs. Outputs are the goods, products, or services that the project delivers to the beneficiaries. Outputs are usually tangible and are generated by using and transforming inputs through project activities. The project's management scope is defined by the outputs, as, by definition, project management cannot extend beyond outputs. There is a close relationship between inputs and outputs; therefore, the DMF cannot list outputs for which there are no inputs (Box 1). Before project approval, project teams assign a percentage weight for each DMF output indicator—based on their criticality to achieving and/or contribution to the project's outcome, cost, or other priorities—and input these into ADB's portfolio management system. The percentage weights form part of ADB's project performance rating methodology used during project implementation (footnote 2).

Outcomes. Outcomes represent the purpose of the project and should describe the immediate and direct benefits of output use or application. Outcome statements should articulate the change that the project is expected to achieve (Box 2). The DMF contains one outcome statement which may have several different dimensions of performance, such as "improved water security and mobility in City A." Performance indicators are then used to measure specific dimensions of the project outcome (Section II.B). For example, assuming women's mobility is an important part of the outcome, this dimension would be measured through a specific performance indicator.

Table 1: Differences Among Results Levels

Results Level	Relationship to Project	Source of Result	Timing of Achievements	Control by Project or Beneficiaries	Accountability	Changes During Project Implementation
Impact (not part of results chain)	Aligned with project outcome	Higher-level documents, e.g., regional, national, subnational, or sector plans or strategies	Usually post project	Outside beneficiary control	No direct project accountability	Should not change, although additional impact statements can be added to reflect alignment with a new strategy or plan introduced after project approval
Outcome (part of the DMF results chain)	Directly influenced by project	Needs of beneficiaries	By end of first full year of operation following physical completion, or before financial closure of project	Within the control of beneficiaries	Project accountable for outcome achievement Project success (i.e., effectiveness criteria) is measured against outcome targets	Major change in scope if there is a material change in the outcome Minor change in scope if changes to the indicators do not materially alter or fundamentally affect the approved project scope and outcome
Output (part of the DMF results chain)	Produced or delivered by project	Project deliverables	By project or TA completion date	Within control of project, given inputs, risks, and critical assumptions	Project accountable for outputs	Minor change in scope if no effect on the outcome

DMF = design and monitoring framework, TA = technical assistance.

Box 1: Output Tips

(i)   Include major products and deliverables of the project.

(ii)   Ensure that, together, outputs will be sufficient to achieve the outcome, given the risks and assumptions. Include an output for each set of activities, except project management activities, which do not produce an output. Phrase outputs in the past tense as already achieved, e.g., "rural roads constructed in the southern districts." Include a word signifying completion (e.g., constructed, rehabilitated, established, implemented, improved) in the statement. Outputs should be fully consistent with the cost estimates and financing plan, and the project definition in schedule 1 to the loan or grant agreement.

(iii)   Do not include any cause-and-effect links. Output statements should not use the words "through," "by," or "in order to" because these words imply cause-and-effect links.

(iv)   Review relationship between outputs and output indicators. If the output statement includes several distinct outputs, consider splitting it into more than one output statement.

Assessment of the project's effectiveness is based on whether the project's intended outcome has been achieved and is attributable to the achieved project outputs. To ensure that outcome performance data will be available in time for completion reporting, the project team should plan the achievement of the outcome indicator within the first year of project operation following physical completion, or before financial closing.[3]

---

[3]   A sovereign project is deemed complete when all its outputs are completed (i.e., when its facilities are completed and ready to operate regardless of the closure of its financial account). Project Administration Instruction 6.06 provides instructions on the timing of project completion report (PCR) preparation and circulation (ADB. 2024. Project Completion Report for Sovereign Operations. *Project Administration Instructions.* PAI 6.06).

For projects with nonphysical outputs, the outcome indicator target dates should be set to ensure that achievement can be assessed in the completion report.

Impacts. The project's results chain is aligned with impact statements, which are sourced from the most relevant strategic document(s), usually a government's national, sector, subnational, or regional plan or strategy, before the project is conceptualized (Box 3). The impact level in the DMF is separated from the results chain to show that its purpose is alignment, not performance measurement. The DMF does not include performance indicators or targets to measure impact statements.[4] Impacts are long-term in nature and are expected to occur sometime after project closing. The timing of expected impacts also varies. For example, a project that takes 6 years to build new transmission lines would make some contribution to the growth of businesses that use electricity only after several years of operation.

Impact statements are restated from the source document to conform to DMF results statement phrasing. One should phrase the impact as achieved, for example, "income, jobs, and business activity increased" and include a change word in the sentence. An impact statement should not include more than one level of cause-and-effect links. Be careful not to choose an impact statement that is too high-level, such as "inclusive economic growth achieved" or "poverty reduced." A statement of this nature is too general to show alignment with the project. In rare cases where there is no relevant official document to cite or paraphrase (e.g., for some TA or in the case of disaster and emergency response projects), the impact(s) can be exclusively defined by the project and "(project defined)" is stated after the impact statement. In other cases, the second and third impact statements can be "project defined."

Table 2 contains sample output, outcome, and impact statements for operations in common ADB areas of sovereign programming.

The DMF includes two other levels: activities and inputs (Figure 2).

Activities. Activities are the groups of tasks carried out using project inputs to produce the desired outputs. The DMF should only include activities whose completion represents important milestones that will allow implementation

Box 2: Outcome Tips

(i) Include only one outcome statement describing the immediate and direct benefits from using or applying outputs.

(ii) Phrase the outcome in the past tense as already achieved, e.g., "increased mobility of rural residents." The statement must include at least one change word (e.g., increased, improved, enhanced).

(iii) Do not include any cause-and-effect links. Outcome statements should not use the words "through," "by," or "in order to." In the following examples, cause-and-effect links are removed: corporate performance improved, graduation rates increased, crop yields improved.

Box 3: Impact Tips

(i)   Source impact from the most relevant government strategic or planning document published before the project is conceptualized.

(ii) Conform the impact statement to design and monitoring framework results statement phrasing. Phrase the impact in the past tense as already achieved. The statement must include at least one change word (e.g., increased, improved, enhanced).

(iii) Split impact statement if the statement shows two levels of results. Up to three impact statements are allowed.

(iv) Review the impact statement to ensure it directly aligns with the results chain (i.e., outcome and outputs). Impact statement should not have the same level as the outcome statement, or be too high such that the outcome's contribution to impact is unclear.

(v)   Cite the source at the end of the statement and/or in a footnote.

progress to be tracked. For example, key activities for an education project might include "develop science, technology, engineering, and mathematics curricula and train trainers by Q4 2026;" "provide relevant training equipment to five selected technical training institutes by Q3 2025;" and "develop and implement an in-service training program for teachers by Q4 2027."

It is good practice to include project management activities at the end of the activities section of the DMF. The cluster should be titled "project management activities."

---

[4] Although impact-level indicators are not included in the DMF, rigorous impact evaluation can still be carried out using the impact statement(s) and results chain from the DMF. See ADB. 2017. *Impact Evaluation of Development Interventions: A Practical Guide.*

Table 2: Example Results Statements for Operations in Common Areas

Results Level	Urban Transport	Energy Generation	Urban Water Supply	Training of Technical and Vocational Education and Training Teachers	Financial Intermediation
Impact (Long-term end goal, not part of results chain)	Jobs and economic activity increased	Health, education, jobs, and economic activity increased	Waterborne diseases reduced	Workforce skills and productivity increased	Employment in small and medium-sized enterprises increased
Outcome (Immediate and direct benefit of output use)	Travel convenience, safety, and affordability for women and men improved	Consumption of electricity in remote communities increased	Consumption of clean, treated water increased	Quality of technical and vocational education and training (TVET) delivery enhanced	Economically viable small and medium-sized enterprises, managed by women and men, increased
Output (Provided or delivered)	Urban rail system constructed Institutional capacity of Department of Transport strengthened	Off-grid solar energy installations constructed Capacity of residents in remote communities to use and maintain solar energy installations enhanced	Water distribution and treatment facilities in urban areas rehabilitated Institutional capacity of water utility service provider strengthened	TVET teacher knowledge and skills improved Quality and relevance of TVET curriculum improved Technical training institutes upgraded	Financing to microfinance beneficiaries, including women, through intermediaries increased

The activities should summarize routine events and activities of the project implementation team or unit, such as planning, procurement, M&E, and reporting. Activities can also include communicating with stakeholders, providing inputs on strategic and policy issues, and undertaking risk mitigation measures. This cluster can help project team leaders organize project management activities and ensure that a budget is provided for key project management concerns. There is no output associated with the project management activities, so they should not be numbered (Box 4).

Box 4: Activities Tips

(i) List key activities and milestones for each output.

(ii) Link design and monitoring framework activities with "B. Overall Project Implementation Plan" in Section II of the project administration manual.

(iii) Indicate the expected completion date for each activity.

(iv) Group and number activities by the output to which they relate.

(v) Include project management activities as appropriate, such as procuring goods, hiring consultants, reporting, monitoring, evaluation, accounting, and auditing, at the end of the activities row, without a number.

(vi) Include any primary data collection undertaken for the project under project management activities.

(vii) Do not include indicators at the activity level.

(viii) For results-based lending, activities should be priority actions from the program action plan. Policy-based lending does not require activities.

Inputs. Inputs are the main resources that the project uses to undertake the activities and produce the outputs. All financial inputs and in-kind inputs for TA that will be used for project activities should be listed in the DMF. This includes those from ADB, the government, and other financing partners, as applicable (Box 5).

Box 5: Input Tips

(i)   Include a summary of the main financial inputs needed to carry out the activities.
(ii)   Group inputs by financing partner.
(iii)   Include direct cofinancing.
(iv)   For technical assistance, also include in-kind contributions by source (except for regional technical assistance).

All cofinancing administered by ADB (fully or partially), and cofinancing not administered by ADB but for which ADB and the financing partner jointly finance the same contract packages, should be included as an input in the DMF with corresponding outputs. Cofinancing should be listed as a critical assumption in the DMF if a third party will finance and deliver outputs that are necessary to achieve the DMF outcome in parallel through separately administered procurement packages (**Section II.D1**).

1. Common Technical Assistance Results Chains

The TA operations that ADB typically finances can be grouped into three general focuses: providing policy and technical advice; supporting capacity development; and promoting knowledge generation, dissemination, and use. A single TA project design may include one or more of these general focuses.

For TA focusing on providing policy and technical advice, recipient governments consider the advice for adoption and implementation. Figure 4 shows a typical results chain for TA providing policy and technical advice, with a leading outcome indicator measuring preliminary indications of use.

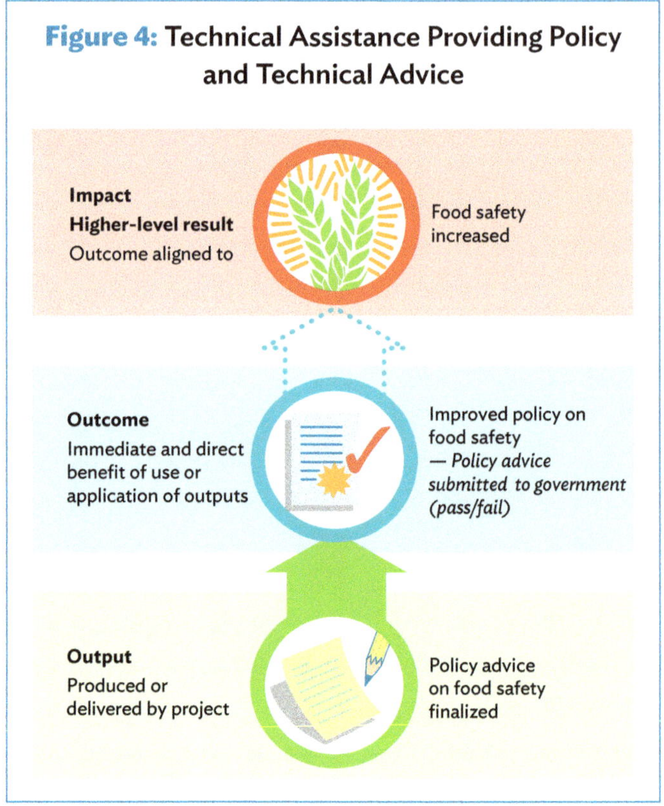

Figure 4: Technical Assistance Providing Policy and Technical Advice

For TA providing capacity development, the results chain is significantly different depending on whether the recipient of capacity development is an organization or individuals (who may be from multiple organizations). The results chain will also differ depending on whether the capacity development involves assistance in implementation. This can be thought of as the difference between "hand over," with no assistance for implementation; and "hand-holding," where implementation is assisted on an ongoing basis. Training is usually a "hand over," while implementation assistance is usually a "hand-holding." Table 3 captures these differences.

Figure 5 shows a typical results chain for a TA providing capacity development, with a leading outcome indicator measuring likelihood of knowledge and skills application.

Some TA projects are concerned with knowledge generation, and its dissemination to and use by a variety of audiences. Figure 6 shows a typical results chain for knowledge dissemination through a conference, with a leading outcome indicator measuring likelihood of application of knowledge.[5]

---

[5]   Indicators for capacity development and knowledge-focused TA projects should measure knowledge and skills enhanced at the output level.

Table 3: Capacity Development Recipients and Implementation Support

Item	No Implementation Support (Hand Over)		With Implementation Support (Hand-Holding)	
	Outputs	Outcome	Outputs	Outcome
Organization recipient	Models, manuals, guidelines, regulations, processes, systems, plans, policies, etc., produced Knowledge and skills enhanced	Models, manuals, etc., applied, implemented, undertaken, enacted, enforced, etc. Knowledge and skills applied	Models, manuals, etc., produced and implemented Knowledge and skills enhanced and applied	Overall performance of organization enhanced
Individual recipients	Knowledge and skills enhanced	Knowledge and skills applied	Knowledge and skills enhanced and applied	Overall performance of individuals enhanced

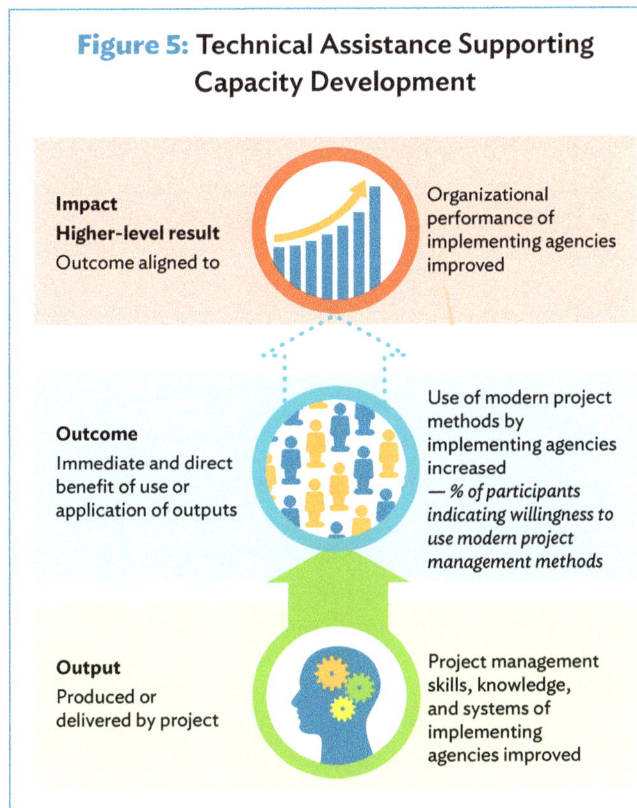

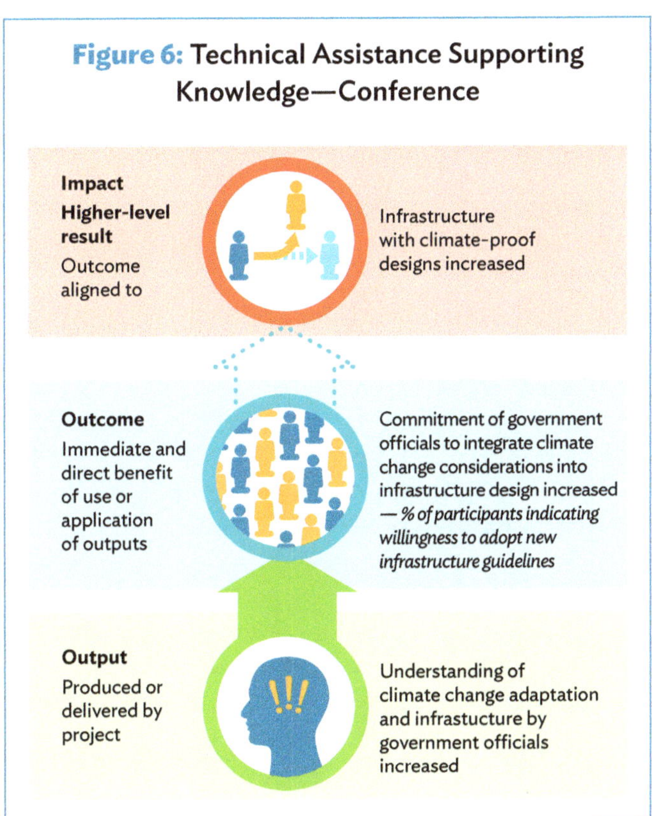

B. Performance Indicators

Results achievement is measured through performance indicators, which include targets to define success. Indicators clarify the expected results and determine their status using quantitative or qualitative measures (Box 6).

Performance indicators provide a measurable basis for project M&E. Key stakeholders should be involved in the selection of indicators and targets to ensure that these are ambitious yet realistic and reflect the needs of the intended beneficiaries.

Box 6: Tips for Measuring Quality Quantitatively

All indicators should be specified in quantitative terms. However, this does not mean that qualitative measurement cannot take place. Indicators that capture a quantitative dimension but are expressed qualitatively can be developed to provide a better understanding of the needs of intended beneficiaries. For example, beneficiary satisfaction with government service is inherently qualitative and measures can be expressed quantitatively. A quantitative indicator could be "Share of residents satisfied or highly satisfied with solid waste management services increased to at least 80% by 2028 (2024 baseline: 56%)" or "At least 85% of residents perceive the safety of roads for pedestrians, cyclists, and motorists has improved by 2028 (2024 baseline: 50%)." Perception indicators are most commonly measured using surveys.

Existing indicators should be used, where possible, to reduce the time and costs required to collect data. This includes indicators for which data are already collected by government agencies, academic institutions, civil society organizations (CSOs), and other sources. However, one should guard against selecting an indicator solely because it already exists. The primary function of an indicator is to measure the result; if the result is not being measured by an existing indicator, a new indicator must be developed.

There are three main types of indicators:

(i)   **Direct indicators** directly measure the subject of interest. For example, the number of fatalities from road accidents annually is a direct indicator of the outcome statement "reduced deaths from road traffic accidents." These are ideal indicators and should be used whenever feasible.

(ii) **Proxy indicators** are indirect measures that approximate to, or are representative of, the subject of interest. They are used to demonstrate change or results where direct measures are not feasible. For example, landlessness or poor housing quality may be used as proxy indicators of poverty. A proxy indicator may be used if (a) the subject of interest is qualitative and cannot be measured directly (e.g., living conditions or good governance); (b) the subject cannot be measured within the available resources or timeline (e.g., behavioral change); and/or (c) it is better value for money to use a proxy indicator because a high-quality one exists.

(iii) **Leading indicators** measure preliminary indications of an outcome by measuring progress along the pathway of change. They provide evidence of something that typically needs to hold true or to occur for the desired outcome to be achieved but are not direct evidence of the outcome itself. For example, the number of workshop participants indicating their willingness or ability to apply the new skills they have learned is a leading indicator for their actual application of the skills.

2. Selecting Performance Indicators

Each indicator must have a baseline and a target. The baseline is the most recent status of performance while the target represents the expected level of achievement. All indicators must be specified quantitatively, as in the following example: Journey from city station A to city station W by public transport reduced to less than 1 hour by 2025 (2020 baseline: at least 2 hours).

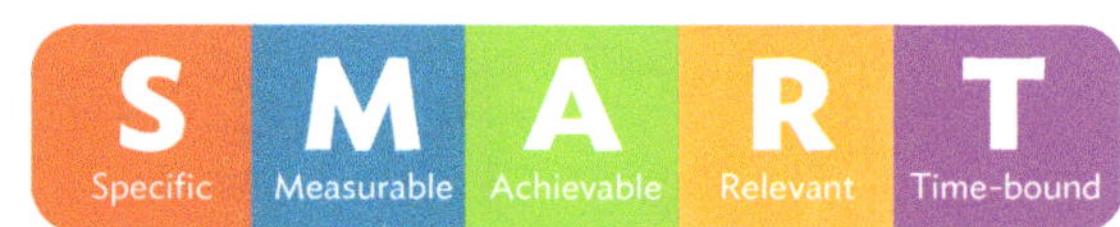

Example

Journey from city station A to city station W by public transport reduced to less than 1 hour by 2025 (2020 baseline: at least 2 hours).

A good performance indicator meets the "SMART" criteria:

(i)   **Specific**—details the outputs or outcome the project seeks to achieve by specifying dimensions, such as who, where, when, quality, quantity, and cost.

(a)   Be specific about who is benefiting by including details such as beneficiaries' sex (male/female), location (urban/rural), socioeconomic status, ethnicity, age, and any other relevant qualities. Ensure indicators that count people are always sex-disaggregated (Box 7).

(b)   Ensure relevant stakeholders understand the indicator. Avoid subjective terms such as "access" or "successful." Instead, define exactly how the output or outcome will be measured. For example, instead of "education management information system successfully in use by Ministry of Education," restate it as "Ministry of Education uses education management information system to generate regular quarterly reports."

Box 7: **Measuring Progress in Gender Equality**

Each Asian Development Bank project is categorized into one of four gender mainstreaming categories. Requirements for a project to be categorized *gender equality objective* include that its design and monitoring framework must have an explicit gender equality outcome statement, and at least one gender-specific outcome-level performance indicator, with at least 50% of outputs including gender performance indicators. Projects categorized *effective gender mainstreaming* must include gender performance indicators for at least 50% of outputs. Projects are categorized *some gender elements* if they include at least one gender performance indicator in less than 50% of outputs. Projects that do not meet these requirements will be categorized *indirect gender benefits*.

(ii) **Measurable**—stated in quantifiable terms (e.g., % of children) and feasible to collect data in time to report in the project completion report (PCR) and in project progress reports as relevant.
  (a) Use indicators that are industry standard for the sector or issue, if available and practical.
  (b) Where possible and appropriate, use indicators for which data are already collected, but do not use an indicator solely because it already exists. If there is no preexisting relevant indicator, seek to identify an indicator for which data can be collected using information systems that are already in place.
  (c) Keep in mind that collecting new data may require data collection activities that have an added cost. These should be planned and budgeted for.
(iii) **Achievable**—realistic about what is to be achieved. The collective judgment of key stakeholders is needed to choose a target that is ambitious, yet realistic (e.g., is a differential in immunization rates between poor/non-poor and male/female children of no more than 10% by 2026 realistically achievable?).
(iv) **Relevant**—appropriate to the results statement it measures and useful for management information purposes. (This requires management judgment: will knowing the share of children under 12 years that are completely immunized be useful for managing the project or assessing its success?)
(v) **Time-bound**—stated with a target and baseline, both with dates (e.g., 80% by 2026; 2020 baseline: urban average 72%, urban poor people 53%, urban non-poor people 80%).

To be specific, indicators should measure and express quantitatively the various dimensions of a result, as follows:

(i) **Quantity**—how much of the result has been delivered? (e.g., number, percentage, ratio)
(ii) **Quality**—with what quality? (e.g., client satisfaction percentage, quality rating scale, pass/fail, yes/no, error rate, design standards or features in the case of outputs)

(iii) **Timeliness**—when, according to set schedule, and for how long? (e.g., by calendar date, length of time, number of hours to use the service)
(iv) **Location**—where are the results located geographically? (e.g., village, state, region)
(v) **With whom**—which groups are involved? (e.g., ethnic groups, women, people living below the poverty line)
(vi) **Cost**—at how much cost per unit? (e.g., $ per child immunized, $ per kilometer (km), $ per application processed)

3. Collecting Baseline Data and Setting Targets

Baseline data should reflect the most recent status of performance. If a project starts in 2024, the baseline data should be for the most recent year, ideally 2023. TA can be used to collect baseline data. Figure 7 shows the relationship between target, performance, and baseline.

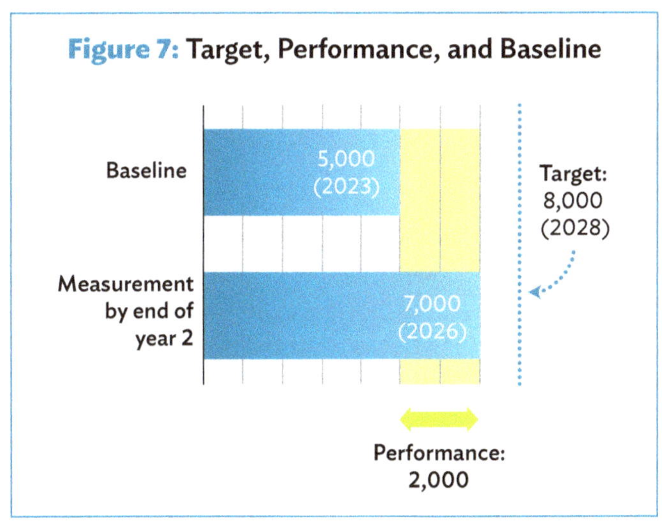

Figure 7: Target, Performance, and Baseline

Four different types of baselines can be used for an indicator and all indicators must have one of these baselines:

(i) **Cumulative baselines** are usually used for outcomes in which additional units will be added to an existing stock or when existing performance can be measured; for example, "Share of residents satisfied or highly satisfied with solid waste management services increased to at least 80% by 2028 (2023 baseline: 56%)."

(ii) **Zero baselines** are usually used for outputs when a project is starting from nothing and adding units; for example: "250 km of road upgraded by 2028 (2023 baseline: 0 km)."

(iii) **Binary baselines** are usually used in policy-based lending when something is to be adopted, approved, or operationalized; for example, "Transport master plan for capital city adopted by city council in 2025 (2023 baseline: drafted)." This type of baseline is recorded quantitatively in ADB's portfolio management system as 0 and its associated target, once achieved, is recorded as 1, hence the term "binary."

(iv) **Not applicable.** "NA" (i.e., not applicable) is used for outputs or outcome when a result is the first of its kind, there is nothing to measure against, and the baseline does not exist; for example, "100% of proposals reviewed by investment board by 2026 (2023 baseline: NA [investment board does not exist yet])"; or "At least 95% of workshop participants report improved knowledge of e-procurement platform by 2027 (2023 baseline: NA [e-procurement platform not yet developed])."

Each indicator must have quantitative targets. Targets should be set considering the needs of stakeholders, the baseline, and, if available, the benchmarks of comparative performance. If an indicator measures more than one dimension of performance, it will need a baseline and target value for each dimension. For instance, in the following example, both the rural and urban dimensions of performance have a separate baseline and target: "24-hour power supply provided for 100% of urban population and 85% of rural population by 2026 (2020 baseline: urban 65%, rural 53%)."

Output and outcome targets must be quantitative, but they do not have to take a single numerical value. They can be set using a range of options, as shown in Table 4. Box 8 provides tips on formulating performance indicators with targets.

Table 4: Options for Target Setting

Target Type	Examples	Key Features	Use When
1. Numerical	Average speed along north–south roadway increased to 60 kilometers per hour by 2029 (2023 baseline: 20 kilometers per hour average).	A point target that is expected to be reached or exceeded	A precise level of performance can be expected
2. Maintained or increased/ decreased	Level of nitrous oxides in urban air maintained or decreased by 2029 (2023 baseline: 90 micrograms per cubic meter).	A floor or ceiling for desired performance in reference to the baseline	The current level of performance is satisfactory, performance improvements are also desirable, but no target amount can be set
3. At least	Staff with malaria prevention accreditation increased to at least 90%, 100% for female staff by 2027 (2023 baseline: 78%, 55% [female]).	A floor for desired performance that does not reference the baseline	A minimum level of target performance can be set and the desired performance trajectory is upward
4. No more than	Road accident response time reduced to no more than 20 minutes by 2028 (2023 baseline: 60 minutes).	A ceiling for desired performance that does not reference the baseline	A minimum level of target performance can be set and the desired performance trajectory is downward
5. On time or on schedule	By 2026, annual audited financial statements published online by 15 July (2023 baseline: at least 6 months late).	A point target that is set with reference to a future date or time	Expected performance is time- or calendar-based
6. Maintained	By 2025, annual operations and maintenance cost recovery maintained at the 2020 level (2020 baseline: 105%).	Baseline performance is to be sustained A range can also be specified, e.g., 100%–130%	The current level of performance is satisfactory and no improvement is expected

Box 8: **Tips for Performance Indicators**

(i) Include at least one indicator for each output and outcome. No indicators are included in the design and monitoring framework for impacts.

(ii) Align the indicator directly with the output or outcome. Ensure that the indicators do not measure the next or previous level of result and that together they measure all dimensions of the corresponding result statement.

(iii) Use stakeholder input where appropriate, especially from beneficiaries, to specify indicators and set targets.

(iv) State the baseline for each dimension of performance measured by the indicator: current performance level, zero, or not applicable.

(v) Specify a target for each dimension of performance measured by the indicator using one of the six target types. Disaggregate any indicator that measures people into female and male for baselines and targets, and ensure targets are supported by the findings of the gender analysis.

(vi) Specify indicators quantitatively, even if measuring qualitative dimensions.

(vii) Limit the number of indicators by including only "need to know" indicators and avoiding "nice to know" indicators.

(viii) Use relevant existing indicators where possible but ensure timely data will be available for monitoring and reporting.

C. Data Sources and Reporting

For each performance indicator, the DMF must record (i) the title of the report or document that will contain the data about the indicator; (ii) the name of the issuing organization; and (iii) how frequently the data will be made available (e.g., monthly, annually, biennially) (Box 9). For websites, state "website data" and footnote the website address. For indicators that require primary data to be collected by the project, also record the data collection method or tool in the DMF; for example, "survey of workshop participants" or "survey of beneficiary households" (Box 10).

Box 10: **Tips for Common Data Collection Methods**

There is no single best way to collect or retrieve data. The most appropriate data collection method is one that yields the most valid and credible data for the indicator and is feasible given resource availability and time constraints. For some indicators, it may be worth collecting the data using more than one method or source to cross-verify the findings and yield more detail, greater accuracy, and thus validity. Consult subject-matter experts and key stakeholders when choosing methods. Common data collection methods for design and monitoring framework indicators include the following:

(i) **Reviews of existing official documents and data.** This includes sources such as management information systems, administrative data, and official statistical databases.

(ii) **Observation.** This involves direct observation or assessment by a qualified expert or experts; for example, the level of participation by women in official meetings is observed and assessed by a gender specialist; the application of skills on the job is observed and assessed by a supervisor.

(iii) **Information from individuals or groups.** This includes key informant interviews, focus group interviews, or a panel of experts; surveys (web-based, handwritten, or verbal face-to-face); and mobile data collection. These are ideally administered both pre- and post-project. They can also be administered once at the end of the project; in which case they need to include questions that reconstruct the baseline if no comparable baseline data already exist.

(iv) **Physical measurements.** Methods in this category are based on agreed indicators and measurement procedures and include measuring geographical information or biophysical changes (e.g., incidence of flooding, incidence of illness, or pollution levels).

Box 9: **Tips for Data Sources and Reporting**

(i) Be as specific as possible about the data source and reporting mechanism. Simply noting "project completion report" is too general. The appropriate data source is critical for collection of valid, quality data; and the design and monitoring framework is meant to be instructive and helpful to those responsible for data collection and reporting.

(ii) For all indicators, include the document name, author, and frequency of publication.

(iii) Number each data source or reporting mechanism to correspond to the applicable indicator.

(iv) Budget for each primary data collection process. Include outcome-level primary data collection, or primary data collection for new indicators, under project management activities.

(v) Data collected about beneficiaries should be disaggregated at least into male and female, and other groups as relevant.

Primary data are collected by the project itself while secondary data are collected by a third party, such as a government department, academic institution, international organization, or CSO. The data collection activities required to collect primary data, such as conducting a survey of beneficiaries, should be included in project management activities and adequately budgeted for. The timing of primary data collection and the responsibility for undertaking it must also be determined. These roles, responsibilities, and associated deliverables should be detailed in the project administration manual and consultants' terms of reference.

Primary data can be collected using a range of methods, including document or administrative data review, literature review, interviews, focus group discussions, surveys and/or questionnaires, expert panel advice, on-site observation, and equipment readings.

When developing a data collection strategy there are several factors to consider in determining what to measure and how to measure it, including representativeness, bias, and attrition.[6]

D. Assumptions and Risks

The outputs and outcome depend, to some extent, on economic, political, social, behavioral, financial, environmental, and institutional factors for their achievement. These factors can be classified as assumptions or risks and should be included in the DMF if they critically affect the results chain.

Good project design involves identifying clear, valid assumptions and risks. Assumptions and risks fill in the cause-and-effect gaps between results levels; they fit between the activities and outputs, and outputs and outcome. Figure 8 depicts the logical sequence of assumptions and risks in the results chain. A useful approach for thoroughly identifying assumptions and risks is to build out the project's theory of change (ToC) (**Section III.D**).

Registering assumptions and risks in the design and monitoring framework. The DMF should contain at least one critical assumption or risk at the output level, and at least one critical assumption or risk at the outcome level.

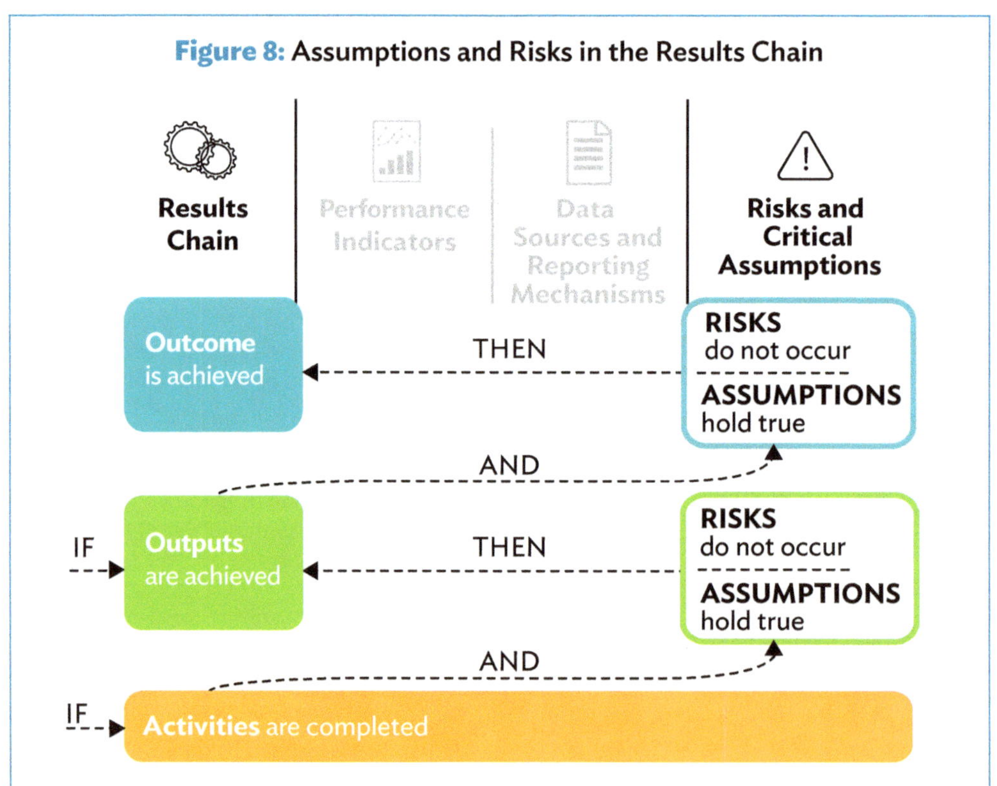

Figure 8: Assumptions and Risks in the Results Chain

---

[6]   For further guidance, see ADB. 2017. *Impact Evaluation of Development Interventions: A Practical Guide.*

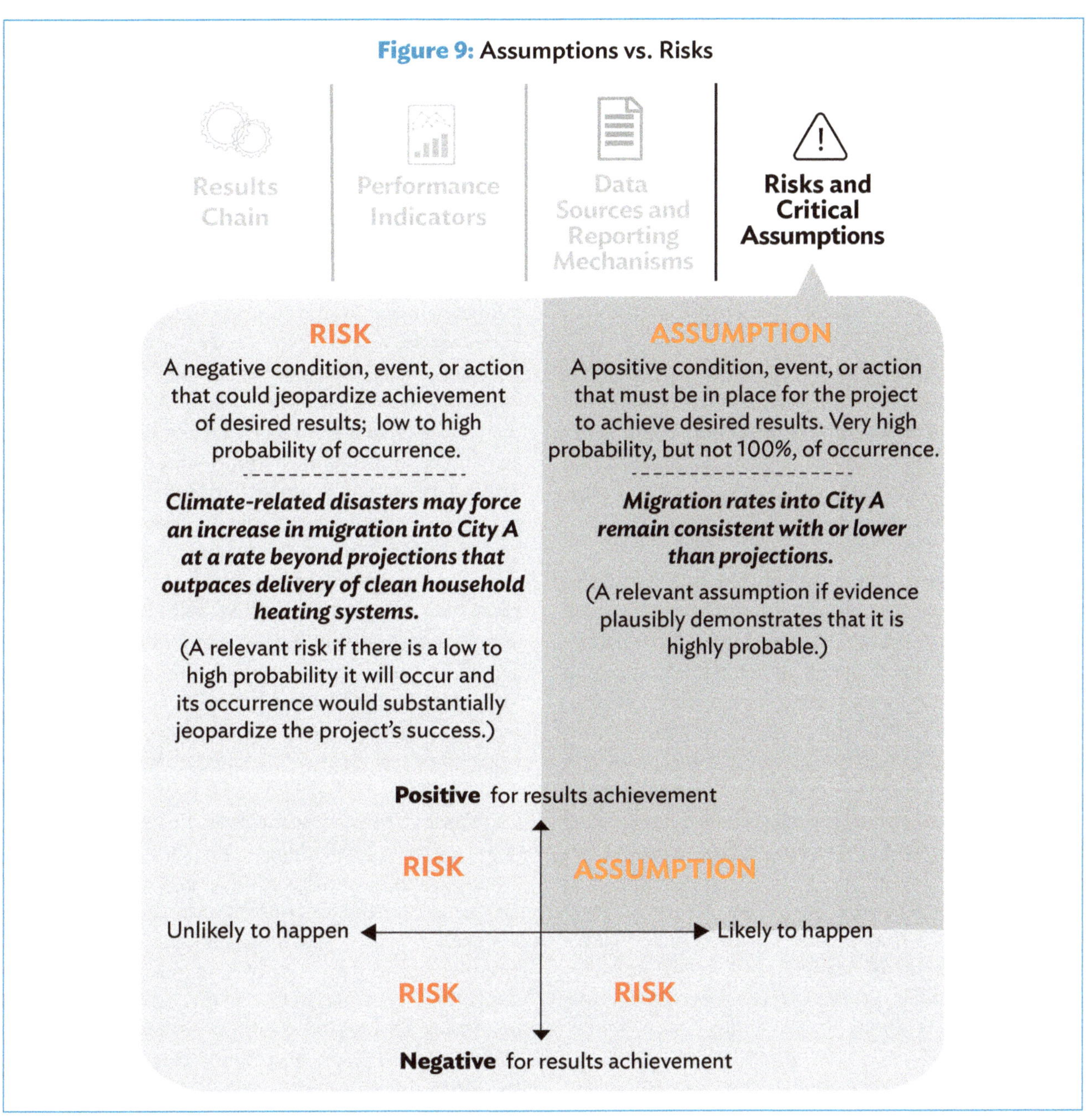

Assumptions vs. risks. The processes for identifying critical assumptions and risks are similar in that they involve asking the question, "What conditions or factors might prevent the project from achieving the desired results?" However, a risk is not simply the negative restatement of an assumption. The distinction between the two concepts is summarized in Figure 9, which includes illustrative examples of a potential critical assumption and a risk for a project that will reduce urban air pollution by installing clean heating systems in city households. It would be relevant to include in the DMF either the critical assumption or the risk illustrated in Figure 9, but not both.

1. Assumptions

Assumptions are the positive conditions, events, or actions that are expected to occur, although not with 100% certainty, and are required for the achievement of the project's planned results. All project results chains are based on assumptions. The higher up the results chain, the more assumptions there are. This is because project stakeholders have a higher level of control and influence on inputs, activities, and outputs than on outcomes and impacts. When an assumption fails to hold, results may be compromised. Analyzing and stating critical assumptions can improve project design by helping identify additional inputs, activities, or outputs that should be included in the design to best ensure it achieves development results and to set output and outcome targets that are realistic. Analyzing assumptions also helps identify project risks.

Identifying assumptions. Assumptions can be divided into two general types: external factors, including assumptions for partner financing, and those relating to the internal cause-and-effect logic of the project's results chain. To identify assumptions, consider the following questions:

(i)   What are we assuming will happen for our planned activities to lead to our outputs, and for our planned outputs to lead to our desired outcome?
(ii)   What conditions must be in place to achieve our desired results? Of these, which are we unsure will be in place in time to achieve the desired results?

External assumptions. Often, assumptions relate to the context within which key project stakeholders will work to achieve targeted results. For example, most ADB-supported projects are designed under the assumptions that there will be continued economic, social, climatic, and political stability within the project environment, and government priorities will remain unchanged over the planning and implementation periods. As these are general assumptions that apply to most projects, it is not helpful to include them in the DMF. However, each of these general types of external assumptions merits closer consideration by the project team to identify project-specific critical external assumptions that warrant inclusion in the DMF; for example, related to climatic and social stability, "Migration rates into City A remain consistent with or lower than projections" (**Figure 9**).

Assumptions for partner financing. Parallel cofinancing that is not administered by ADB is an important factor outside the project's control that often helps achieve the outcome. For example, an ADB-supported water project may install a piped water distribution system (output) but not the household connections (second output) needed for households to use the treated water. However, another development partner may be providing financing to connect households. If the outcome of the ADB-supported project is "household consumption of treated water increased," the ADB-supported project outputs, together with the outputs financed by the other partner(s), should be sufficient to achieve this outcome. When these other outputs are not administered by ADB, and are financed in parallel, but are needed for the ADB-supported project to reach its outcome, they should be recorded as an assumption in the DMF along with the name of the financier. For example, "World Bank Group installs water supply connections to 250,000 households."

Assumptions about the internal cause-and-effect logic of the project's results chain. These important links implicit within the project's results chain often relate to human behavior or the technical feasibility of project plans. For example, a project for which the output statement is "teachers' skills improved" and the outcome statement is "students receive improved quality of teaching" assumes that the teachers trained will subsequently be willing and able to apply what they have learned in the classroom. This assumption is a critical link in the pathway of change between the project's outputs and outcome. These types of assumptions merit questioning because the project should be designed to rely on the smallest number of critical assumptions possible. Critical assumptions about the internal cause-and-effect logic of a project's results chain should be based on evidence. Evidence should be cited in the report and recommendation of the President (RRP), with clear reference to studies and comparable contexts in which the cause-and-effect logic has been demonstrated.

Registering critical assumptions. Assumptions for partner financing must be identified in the DMF while including any other assumptions critical to project success is optional. An assumption is considered critical when the project will likely not work as planned and may fail to achieve its intended results if it does not hold true. **Figure 10** provides a decision tree to help identify critical assumptions. In addition to identifying critical assumptions in the DMF, it is also a good practice to identify and explain them in the section of the RRP that describes the project's design, and include them as conditions in loan covenants, as relevant, to ensure they hold true.

2. Risks

Risks are factors that can hinder progress from one result level to the next. They are potential conditions, events, or actions that would adversely affect or make it difficult to achieve the outputs and outcome, and sustain the outcome. For sovereign operations, all risks are recorded in ADB's risk assessment and risk management plan (RAMP), a supplementary document to the RRP.[7] Risks assigned

---

[7]   OM C4/OP states that the RAMP should address the public financial management, procurement, and corruption risks based on the preliminary assessment in the project concept note. (ADB. 2022. Operations Manual Bank Policies. *Operations Manual.* OM C4/OP.) TA operations do not require a RAMP unless they use transfer of funds as a payment type or disbursement channel.

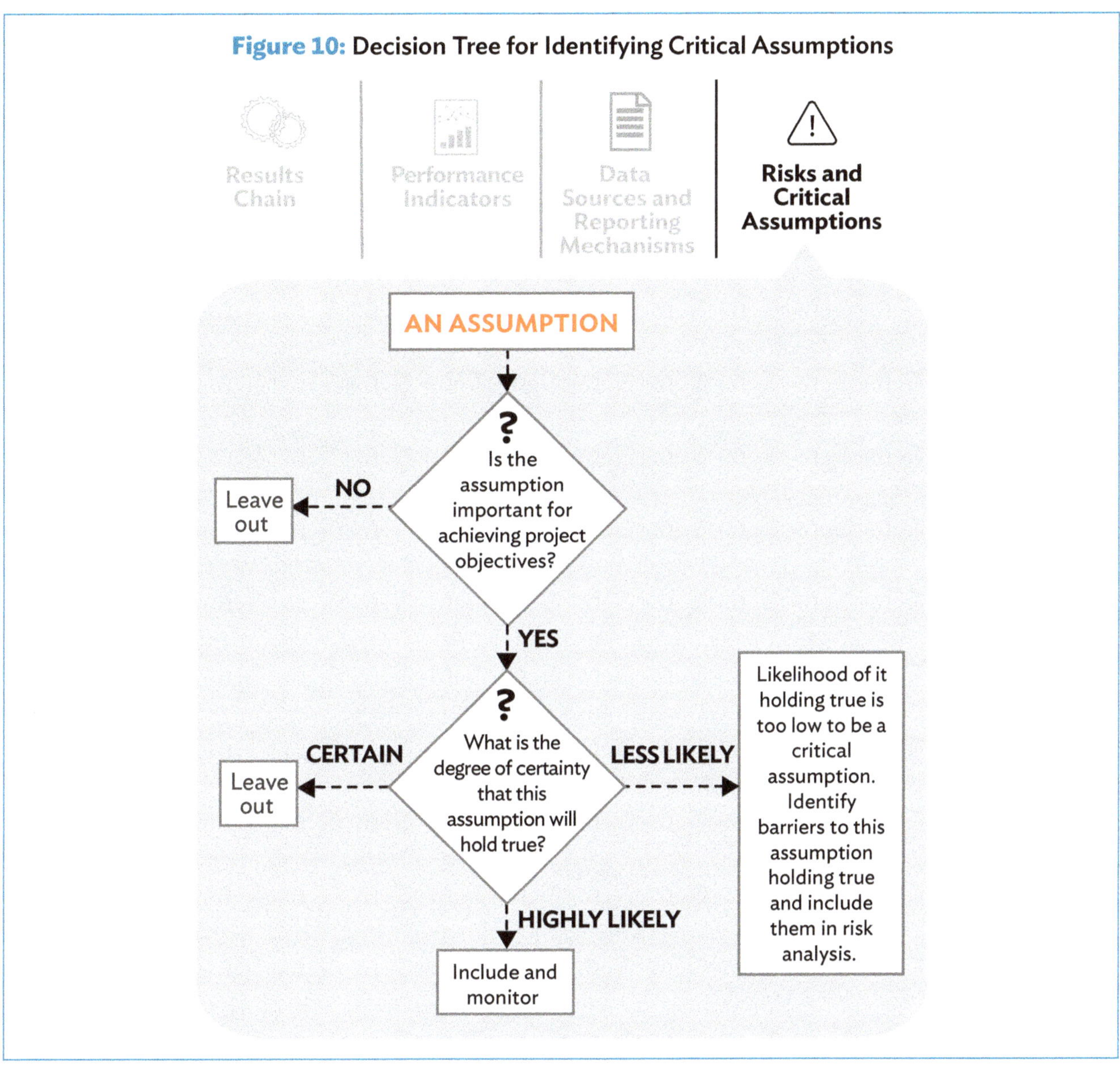

Figure 10: Decision Tree for Identifying Critical Assumptions

ratings of *high* or *substantial* in the RAMP and whose occurrence would have a significant negative effect on the achievement of the outputs or outcome should be stated in the DMF.

Identifying risks. To identify risks, one should consider the following questions:

(i)   What are the forces acting against project success?
(ii) What occurrences or actions might happen at any point in the project cycle that would significantly jeopardize achievement of the intended results?

For example, critical factors affecting the outcome, "Mobility of people and goods between cities A and B increased" include deteriorating security conditions, adverse weather events beyond projected parameters, and deterioration of economic conditions decreases ability to pay for transport. The analysis would be as follows:

(i)   Are security conditions necessary to increase mobility? Yes. Are they likely to remain stable or improve? No. State as risk: "Security conditions in rural areas deteriorate."
(ii) Would adverse weather events beyond projected parameters affect mobility? Yes. Are they likely to happen? Yes. State as risk: "Storm season is worse than projected."
(iii) Is the decreased ability to pay likely to constrain mobility? Yes. Is it likely to happen? Preparatory studies show that people are able and willing to pay for transport, but there is a medium degree of likelihood

that the country will enter a recession in the coming years, which if it happens, would reduce poor people's ability to pay for transport. State as risk: "Deterioration of economic conditions decreases ability to pay for transport."

A risk should satisfy two conditions to be included in the RAMP: its occurrence must be uncertain, and if it occurs it should negatively affect the achievement of project results. For example, "security conditions" is not a risk; the current state of security is a known fact with no uncertainty. However, "security conditions deteriorate" is uncertain and, therefore, a possible risk. The RAMP should be updated throughout the course of project preparation. Any measure taken or planned that puts a risk within the project's full control, or removes the uncertainty about it, also changes that risk to a fact which should then be removed from the RAMP. A risk that is included as a loan covenant or a project readiness criterion or is eliminated by project redesign should not be included in the RAMP because it has been brought within the project's full control.

Analyzing risks. An analysis of risks is important to understand the constraints that the project may face. Some risks may be important enough to warrant action to mitigate their potential effects. Others, referred to as "killer risks," may require the project to be redesigned or not undertaken. **Figure 11** shows a risk analysis matrix that can be used to categorize risks and select appropriate actions.

Depending on the importance and/or likelihood of the risks occurring, the following actions can be taken:

(i)   **Low:** Accept risk, take no action.
(ii)   **Moderate:** Periodically measure the risk factor, especially for changes in likelihood of occurrence.
(iii) **Substantial and high:** To the extent possible, mitigate effects through design (**Box 11**). Include design measures to reduce the likelihood of occurrence or the effects if the risk occurs and create a contingency plan to deal with the consequences of the risk occurring.
(iv)   **Killer risk:** Redesign the project.

Registering risks. For sovereign operations, all major risks to the project are identified and analyzed in the RAMP. Rate each risk in the RAMP as *high, substantial, moderate,* or *low.* List all *high* and *substantial* risks from the RAMP in a table in the RRP. From this table, identify all risks that would affect achievement of the outputs or outcome and that fit within the vertical logic of the results chain, and include these in the DMF (**Box 12**).

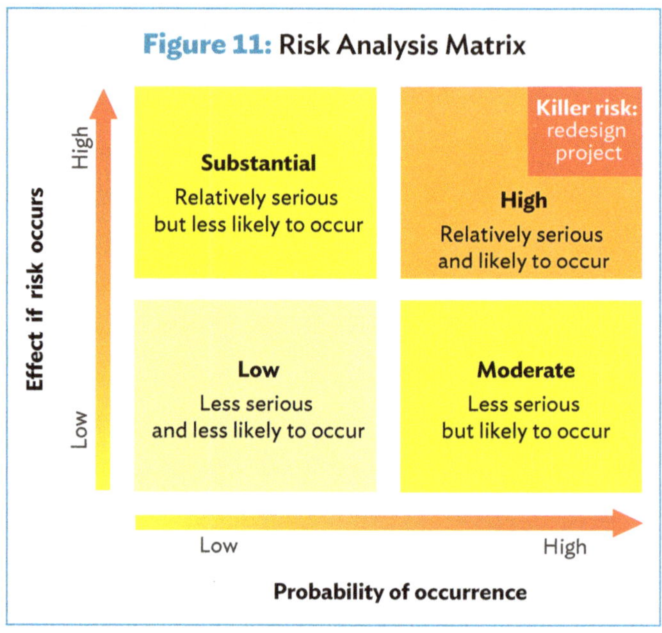

Box 11: Mitigation Tip

Mitigation refers to actions undertaken to reduce or remove the effects of a risk occurring, or the likelihood of occurrence. Mitigation does not remove the risk. The project can only remove the risk through redesign. Not all risks can be mitigated, and when they cannot and the project moves forward, their possible effects are accepted.

Box 12: Risk Tips

(i)   Risks are negative and uncertain.
(ii)   Do not include as risks (a) any factors that the project fully controls, (b) risks included as loan covenants, (c) project readiness criteria, (d) risks already eliminated through redesign, and (e) planned mitigation measures.
(iii) For sovereign operations, list all project risks in the risk assessment and risk management plan. List all *high* and *substantial* risks from the plan in the summary of risks and mitigating measures table in the report and recommendation of the President.
(iv)   In the design and monitoring framework list all high and substantial risks that would affect achievement of the outputs or outcome and fit within the vertical logic of the results chain. Risks can be linked to specific outputs if desired.
(v)   Risks that would threaten delivery of outputs, even if all activities were successfully completed, are listed at the output level in the design and monitoring framework; while risks that would threaten achievement of the desired outcome, even if all outputs were successfully delivered, are listed at the outcome level.

3. Monitoring Critical Assumptions and Risks

Risks and critical assumptions should be monitored closely throughout project implementation. During review missions, project teams should review the risks that may affect the likelihood of achieving DMF targets, reassess the executing and implementing agencies' capacity to mitigate these risks, and document any updates in the back-to-office report and aide memoire.[8] When a planned result is not achieved or problems occur, a faulty assumption is often the cause. Critical assumptions should be reviewed regularly to check if they are still valid and to determine whether new ones have emerged. When project monitoring reveals that a critical assumption is not holding true or a risk has materialized, the design of the project or the project's targeted results should be adjusted.

Analyzing and monitoring assumptions and risks helps identify and monitor unintended outcomes and negative effects. Projects may have unintended positive results that were not identified in the DMF. These can be recorded in a monitoring report and the PCR. Of greater concern, however, are the unintended negative consequences that projects can have. The possibility that these might occur is classified as a risk. Project teams should monitor for unintended negative consequences of the project and devise an action plan to avoid or address these if they arise.

---

[8] ADB. 2024. Project and Technical Assistance Administration Missions. *Project Administration Instructions.* PAI 6.02.

III DESIGN AND MONITORING FRAMEWORK FORMULATION PROCESS

The process used to design a project, including its DMF, is critical to its eventual success. Projects define an agreement between borrowers, intended beneficiaries, and ADB on expected project results and causal links between result levels, risks and critical assumptions, and the indicators and targets that will be used to measure performance. The DMF articulates and communicates the planned performance of the project. Its quality relies on a good design process to ensure that the planned results are achievable and will meet the needs of the intended beneficiaries.

Ideally, all stakeholders (i.e., intended beneficiaries and other parties) should be involved in a participatory process to determine the range of existing problems and decide which of them should be addressed through the project. The stakeholders should also be involved in determining the solutions the project will deliver and the targets the project should achieve. This may include applying approaches such as human-centered design, which involve intended beneficiaries extensively in the design and testing of potential solutions. Regardless of the approach used, a project that is designed in isolation from its intended beneficiaries is more likely to fail.

While the extent of stakeholder participation will vary by project, it is equally important in every project (Box 13). Even projects that have disparate and dispersed beneficiaries, such as those that reform national systems or processes, or large infrastructure projects such as a highway, a wind farm, or a container port, benefit from stakeholder participation. The nature of these projects makes beneficiary consultation more challenging. However, the siting, construction, and operation of infrastructure often affect local populations, and, therefore, at the very least, the projects benefit from stakeholder consultation to reduce localized negative effects. In addition, design modifications can ensure some benefits accrue to poor people or marginalized groups, thus making the project more inclusive.

A project should ideally be conceived through the following five main steps. Steps (i) to (iii) comprise the situation analysis, while steps (iv) and (v) correspond to solution development (Figure 12).

(i)   **Align with country priorities.** Select a key country development outcome from the country partnership strategy (CPS) results framework.[9]

Box 13: Three Reasons Why a Participatory Approach Is Important

(i)   Projects must be designed to respond to the needs of intended beneficiaries (people or organizations) in relevant and appropriate ways. Intended beneficiaries are the most knowledgeable about the problems they face and how their needs can be met. Projects cannot be properly designed to address problems and provide solutions to meet needs without involving the intended beneficiaries and other key stakeholders.

(ii)   Project stakeholders will be more committed to implementing a design they helped create.

(iii) A group process usually produces a higher-quality, more relevant design and monitoring framework, as groups can make better decisions than any one individual. The participatory process could involve the borrower, executing and implementing agencies, other government organizations, civil society organizations, the private sector, intended beneficiaries, and the Asian Development Bank project team and consultants.

---

[9]   For TA, this step may not apply.

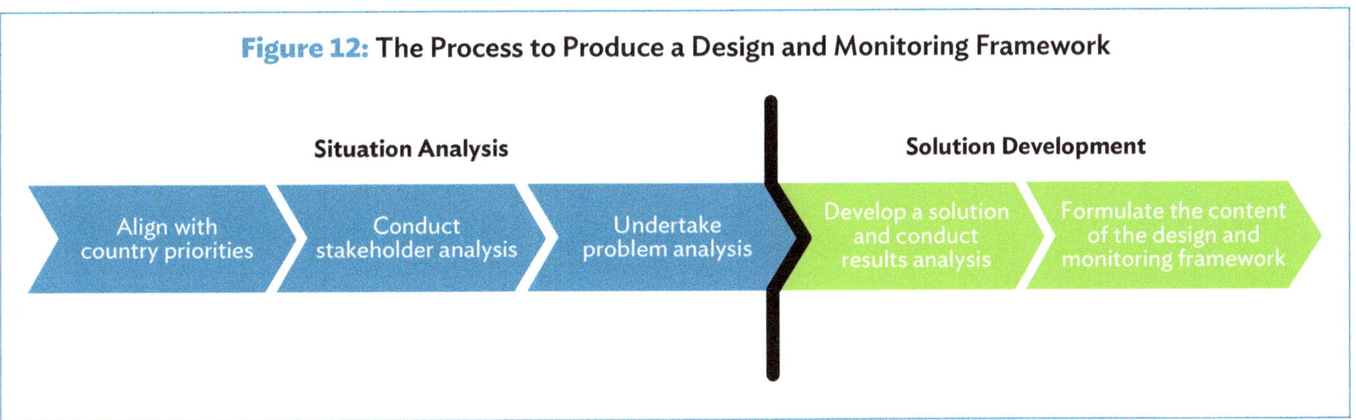

Figure 12: The Process to Produce a Design and Monitoring Framework

(ii) **Conduct stakeholder analysis.** Identify and define the role of stakeholders who can significantly influence or are important in a particular context, for example, a development problem, issue, or sector.

(iii) **Undertake problem analysis.** Identify the development problem(s) to be addressed. In consultation with key stakeholders, identify and analyze the nature and underlying causes of the problem(s) and their effects (Box 14). Develop a problem analysis diagram to help conduct a thorough problem analysis and visually communicate it. This diagram is required for all sovereign operations and is optional for TA.

(iv) **Develop a solution and conduct results analysis.** Identify improvements that may be made within a given time frame and determine the scope of the proposed project, ensuring the design is based on a well-researched theory of change (ToC). A ToC diagram can also be drawn to aid a thorough results analysis and visually communicate it.

(v) **Formulate the content of the design and monitoring framework.** Decide on the DMF results chain and complete the DMF template.

This general process is relevant even in cases where the developing member country (DMC) approaches ADB to finance a project that they have already identified. In these cases, steps (i) to (v) should still be taken to validate the project concept and inform the detailed design. Tips for applying good project design practices within different operational realities are provided throughout this section.

A. Align with Country Priorities

For sovereign operations, the starting point of the analysis should be the summary sector assessment in the CPS and the results framework. This contains key country development outcomes that ADB projects will support.[10] The outcome specified in the DMF should be aligned with a country development outcome in the CPS. However, depending on the project results, the alignment may be closer at the sector output or impact levels. Disaster and emergency response projects are exempted from this step. For TA, the link may be to the summary sector assessment, a regional strategy, or another high-level strategy or plan.

Box 14: Tips for Resourcing a Participatory Design Process

Project teams from the Asian Development Bank (ADB) can draw on several sources of financing to support thorough and participatory situation analysis and solution development for a project. Approved along with the project concept note, technical assistance funds can finance consultants who can support further stakeholder consultation. The consultants might, for example, conduct surveys or facilitate consultation workshops to further expand and validate the initial problem analysis conducted for the concept note and help develop a high-quality design and monitoring framework. Project readiness financing, technical assistance, and some ADB-administered trust funds can also finance these activities even before the project concept note is approved.

---

[10]   If a DMF can link at both the sector outcome and output levels, the link should be specified at the output level. For more details, see ADB. 2022. *Guidelines for Country Partnership Strategy Results Frameworks.*

B. Conduct Stakeholder Analysis

Planning is more effective when it is done with the participation of key stakeholders, and it is therefore important to conduct stakeholder analysis when preparing any project. The primary goal of stakeholder analysis is to assess the needs of affected citizens. The analysis is done during the due diligence phase, and it is good practice to review, reassess, and possibly repeat it at strategic intervals throughout the project cycle.

All projects involve several key stakeholders. In general, stakeholders may be categorized as government, civil society (including citizens and CSOs), and the private sector. Stakeholders are the agencies, organizations, groups, or individuals that have a direct or indirect interest in the project and the development problems it seeks to address. Stakeholders may affect, be affected by, or perceive to be affected by a decision, activity, or result of the project. Key stakeholders of ADB-financed projects vary depending on the project's nature. Common ones include the borrower; the executing agency; the implementing agency; other government agencies at central and local levels; civil society, including nongovernment organizations and advocacy groups; private sector representatives; citizens at large, including intended beneficiaries, marginalized groups, and those potentially negatively affected; and development partners.

Stakeholder analysis is a diagnostic process that enables the project team, working closely with project stakeholders, to identify key stakeholders, including intermediaries and intended beneficiaries, their relationships to each other, and their level of interest in, and influence over, the issues at hand. It helps understand the interests of important and influential stakeholders in relation to development problems, project results, and potential safeguard issues. It also helps identify which groups are supportive and which may oppose the project strategy and subsequently obstruct project implementation; it also provides a sound basis for taking appropriate actions to gain the support of any opponents and to get key supporters more involved. The findings of stakeholder analysis are the basis for the problem analysis and are used to inform project identification, design (including developing tailored behavior change communication approaches as relevant), and implementation.

Process. Stakeholder analysis includes the following steps:[11]

(i) Based on the issue(s) the project will address, consider the potential geographic areas and beneficiaries that the project could assist. The project could consider, for example, the issues of transport in rural areas, elder care, or urban air quality. Identify all the stakeholders involved in the issue(s), grouping them by category (e.g., intended beneficiary groups, public sector organizations, CSOs, advocacy groups, private sector, and development partner agencies). Be sure to distinguish among the different subsections of the stakeholder group as relevant to the context. Specifically, it is important to identify marginalized groups and subgroups; for example, a population of older people may need to be differentiated by caste, ethnicity, and/or gender.

(ii) Determine the interests of each group with reference to each issue (e.g., elder care, youth skills development, inclusion of people with disabilities). Record how and why they are involved, the level of intensity of their interests and concerns, their expectations, and their potential to benefit or suffer as a result of any changes to the context or situation surrounding the issue.

(iii) Determine which problems each group perceives surround each issue (e.g., What are the problems associated with elder care?). Record clear problem statements that describe the effects on those affected (e.g., for the issue of transport in rural areas, the problem should be stated as "travel is long, uncomfortable, and expensive" [correct]; rather than "no road maintenance system" [incorrect]).

(iv) Identify the resources—financial and nonfinancial—each group has put, or could raise, toward each issue. This includes resources to support or prevent change. Formal organizations have both financial and nonfinancial resources, while population and civil society groups have predominantly nonfinancial resources. These can include labor, political influence, votes, readiness to strike, and public pressure.

(v) List the mandates or formal authority that stakeholders must carry out in a particular function, as appropriate. Generally, population groups, such as low-income groups, farmers, and women, do not have mandates.

Various tools can support project teams in conducting this process, including a simple stakeholder analysis table (**Figure 13**), which is useful for compiling and communicating the information for each step.

---

[11] For detailed guidance and tools for effectively engaging stakeholders throughout the project cycle consult ADB. 2021. *A Sourcebook for Engaging with Civil Society Organizations in Asian Development Bank Operations.*

Figure 13: Stakeholder Analysis Table Template

Stakeholder (i)	Stakeholder's Interest (ii)	Perceived Problems (iii)	Resources (iv)	Mandate (v)

Steps (ii) to (v) are best done using a participatory process. Suitable approaches range from basic consultations and focus group discussions to more hands-on brainstorming sessions and workshops. The project team should use its judgment to determine which is most appropriate, bearing in mind that the main objective is to identify all key stakeholders, accurately capture their interests and perspectives, and help secure their support. Practical factors to consider include the cost of workshops and alternative means of communication, support to ensure the inclusion of women, availability of local licensed group facilitators or moderators, and time constraints. At a minimum, the process should include representatives of different stakeholder groups identified by the borrower, project team, and resident mission.

To reach out to beneficiaries and communities effectively, ADB typically works with CSOs to organize workshops and consultations. The CSOs' familiarity with local communities and their expertise in participatory approaches make them suitable organizers of community-based consultations. Representatives of marginalized groups bring experience and specialized participatory skills that are valuable for ensuring effective inclusion, particularly of marginalized groups (e.g., women facilitators and youth in peer-to-peer focus group discussions). Workshops should be led by an experienced facilitator. The workshops can include mixed groups of stakeholders or representatives of a single group. If there are power dynamics that may prevent certain groups from expressing their views, then it is best to hold workshops with these groups separately, at least initially (Box 15).

There is a tendency, especially in the case of large projects with disparate and dispersed beneficiaries, for planning teams not to involve certain stakeholders in the planning process. It is important to ensure consultations follow the principles of consensus building and conflict resolution,

Box 15: Tips for Conducting Participatory Stakeholder Consultations

(i)   Select stakeholders that adequately represent relevant groups and sectors.

(ii)   Ensure participants are informed about the topics and issues for discussion in advance of the consultation. Provide briefing materials as early as possible and in a language the stakeholders understand.

(iii)   Manage expectations and clarify upfront with participants which areas are to be covered by the consultation.

(iv)   After the consultation, give stakeholders feedback about how their comments have been considered.

(v)   Although civil society organizations are the usual intermediaries for reaching citizens, it may also be possible to consult citizens through other means such as social media or other forms of technology.

and that representatives consulted adequately represent the various interest groups. Make sure to include the following groups:

(i)   **Marginalized groups.** These groups are often left out on the assumption that they are not well enough informed or educated to be able to contribute. Leaving out these groups, who are often the main intended beneficiaries of projects, is a costly mistake. Consequences include less relevant project design and implementation challenges later. Remember the motto, "Nothing about us without us," and avoid missing key stakeholders by asking, "Whose voice is not normally heard on this issue?" Project teams should take proactive steps to engage women's organizations, both formal and informal, and to involve women from marginalized groups during consultations and focus group discussions.

(ii) **Groups who might have negative or opposing views on the development issue or project strategy.** These groups have the potential to obstruct the project. Involving them in project design is important to ensure their concerns are heard and considered early on and to increase the likelihood that they will accept and subsequently support the project.

(iii) **Groups essential to project sustainability.** Include stakeholders who may not be involved in project implementation but might be involved after the project has been completed, such as agencies or groups that will operate and maintain project outputs. Involving these stakeholders in the design is critical for ensuring the sustainability of the project's results.

Stakeholder analysis and engagement should continue throughout the project cycle because it fulfills different functions at different stages. During problem identification, it serves to identify important and influential stakeholders and draws attention to how to involve them in the analytical and planning process. During project formulation, it guides design decisions and the analysis of assumptions and risks. During project implementation, it informs strategies to keep stakeholders informed, track their changing circumstances and interests, and plan their possible involvement during implementation.

C. Undertake Problem Analysis

Problem analysis is the second diagnostic process in conducting situation analysis. A thorough problem analysis provides an understanding of the main problems and binding constraints (e.g., economic, cultural, sociopolitical, environmental, and gender equality related) surrounding the issue or issues that the project will address; and the causes of the main problems and their effects on the lives of people (including women and men of all ages, ability, socioeconomic status, and ethnicity), communities, and organizations. Once completed, a good problem analysis informs a relevant project design and provides a clear rationale for why it is important to invest in the project.

ADB uses the problem analysis diagram as a tool to support thorough problem analysis and communicate it visually to key stakeholders. This tool is used to (i) analyze the existing situation surrounding an issue or set of issues, (ii) identify the major problems and constraints, and (iii) visualize the cause-and-effect relationship diagrammatically.

Teams can use two main approaches for the diagram:

(i) The diagram can present an in-depth analysis of the major problems and associated constraints related to the issue that the proposed project will focus on (e.g., "technical and vocational education in province A" or "livability of city B"). This type of problem analysis diagram is prepared during the associated reconnaissance mission, and it can be further developed during RRP preparation and associated fact-finding missions.

(ii) Alternatively, the diagram can present a broader analysis of the major problems and associated constraints affecting one or more issue areas or sectors in the DMC or group of DMCs (e.g., "plastic pollution in the oceans of region X," "livability of cities in DMC X," "public financial management in DMC X," or "energy sector in DMC X"). This broader type of problem analysis diagram may have been prepared as part of the country sector assessment.

Various designs can be used to develop a problem analysis diagram. **Figure 14** provides an illustrative example. A good diagram brings clarity to a complex context by illustrating the main problems and cause-and-effect relationship between them. This may include illustrating problems that are mutually reinforcing (i.e., interconnected in a "vicious cycle") by using a double-headed arrow, and using both horizontal and vertical arrows to illustrate causal connections between various problems. There is no minimum or limit to the number of boxes in a diagram. Project teams can decide on the appropriate scope and depth of analysis. Too narrow a scope is of limited analytical value and may oversimplify the issue, leading to an inadequate solution analysis. On the other hand, it is important to keep focused on the main issue area because a focus that is too broad might cause a loss of direction and clarity among stakeholders.

Process. Problem analysis should be undertaken in a participatory manner, in consultation with key stakeholders identified during the stakeholder analysis. Furthermore, stakeholder analysis should continue during the problem analysis stage. When conducting a problem analysis, key questions to ask for each issue explored are: "Who does this affect most?," "Who controls or manages this?," "Who decides or is formally responsible for this?," and "Who has the power to change this?." The ADB team is responsible for finding a suitable way to involve the stakeholders effectively, considering the local context. Ideally, the problem analysis diagram is developed during a half- or full-day workshop with key stakeholders, or a series of smaller stakeholder workshops from which the results are merged into a comprehensive diagram.

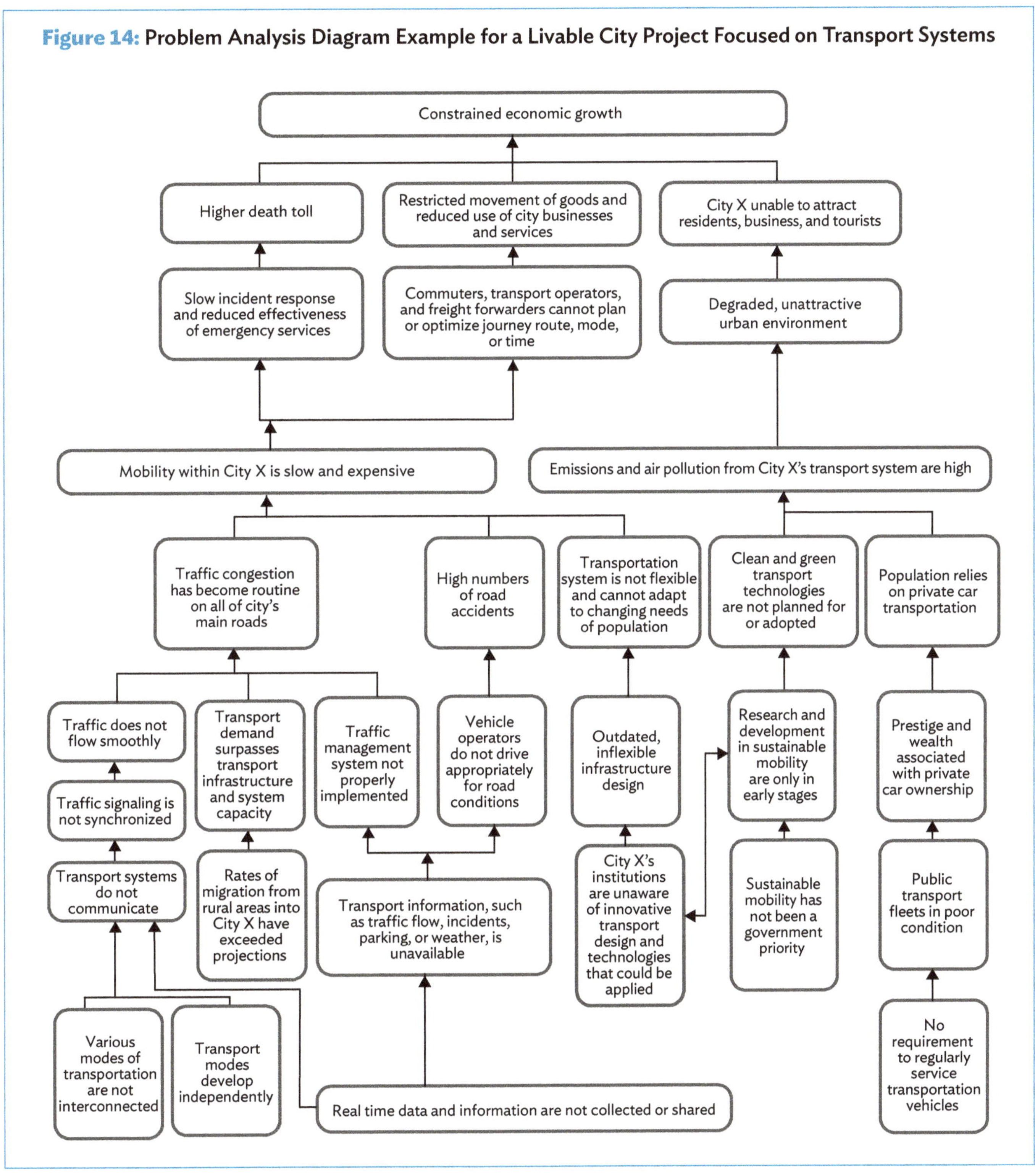

Figure 14: Problem Analysis Diagram Example for a Livable City Project Focused on Transport Systems

A good problem analysis incorporates data and information from different sources. Start with any research and data that already exists, including studies and analyses of the issue, and documentation from previous projects addressing the same or a similar issue, especially evaluation studies. Refer also to key strategic frameworks such as the ADB CPS, or regional, national, subnational, or sector strategies or plans. Complement and validate this document-based information with information collected directly from key stakeholders and subject-matter experts via interviews, meetings, and/or focus groups discussions, and from site observations by the project team.

Box 16: Tips for Applying Good Practices to Suit Operational Realities—Situation Analysis

Sometimes, developing member countries approach the Asian Development Bank to finance a project they have already identified and may also have already designed to some degree. In these cases, the bank's project team should confirm the extent to which the proposed project has been informed by a participatory and evidence-based situation analysis. It is useful to review the stakeholder and problem analyses with key stakeholders to ensure the proposed project and its design are relevant.

A problem analysis diagram can be developed through four main steps (Box 16):

(i) **Identify an initial set of problems surrounding the issue.** Brainstorm a few problems related to the issue, drawing on documented data and information and inputs from key stakeholders. When stating a problem, ensure the following:

    (a) State the problem as a negative condition or reality, not in terms of specific things being unavailable or the solution being absent. For example, stating a problem as "lack of technical and vocational education and training (TVET) institutes in rural areas" formulates the problem in terms of what is missing and may lead to a project being created to build TVET institutes; whereas "a high proportion of rural unemployed youth are not enrolled in educational programs" states a factual problem that could have several underlying causes, including cultural, economic, or other factors such as low level of interest in existing TVET programs among youth. This latter problem statement facilitates a more thorough analysis that can help the team consider a broader range of more relevant solutions.

    (b) Be specific and clear. For example, "rural road maintenance by district road authorities does not meet national quality standards" is better than "poor quality of maintenance."

    (c) Ensure ownership by a stakeholder or group. Problem identification should focus on what is happening and to whom. This should involve discussions about whether specific groups are affected more than others. A good problem statement is described from the perspective of those it affects. For example, "travel in rural areas of the district is time consuming, uncomfortable, and expensive" is better than "suboptimal rural transit;" and "subnational government institutions lack expertise in budget management" is better than "lack of institutional capacity." A helpful guiding question is,

"Are we adequately capturing the specific problems facing institutions and key groups, especially men and women, minorities, and marginalized groups?"

(ii) **Identify direct causes.** Identify the major causes of each problem by asking, "What causes this to happen?" It is often helpful to think in terms of categories of causes, such as policy constraints, institutional constraints, capacity weaknesses, or social or cultural norms. Repeat step (ii) viewing direct causes as problems and asking, "Why has this happened?" Place the direct causes of each of these problems below. Continue to drill down until the analysis is exhausted and specific root causes are identified. The number of problems shown in the diagram is not restricted and will vary based on the nature and complexity of the issue being analyzed. Figure 15 illustrates the question-and-answer logic used to build the diagram.

(iii) **Identify direct effects.** Starting from the problems at the top of the problem analysis diagram, identify the direct effects by asking the question, "What are the effects of this problem?" for each problem statement. Formulate the answer as a problem statement and place it above the problem statement to which it is linked. Continue to specify effects until the final effects are reached.

(iv) **Review and refine.** Refine the problem analysis diagram by reviewing the interrelationships between each problem statement. To check the logic, ask the question, "Why does this occur?" as you move downward from one problem statement to the next. The response should provide a clear direct cause; if there is a major leap in logic, fill in the gap with one or more additional problem statements. It is unlikely that the first formulation of the problem analysis diagram will be correct. Problem statements and cause-and-effect links may need factual verification through research or further consultation with stakeholders or technical experts. Different stakeholders may also need to be consulted as new issues are uncovered during the analysis.

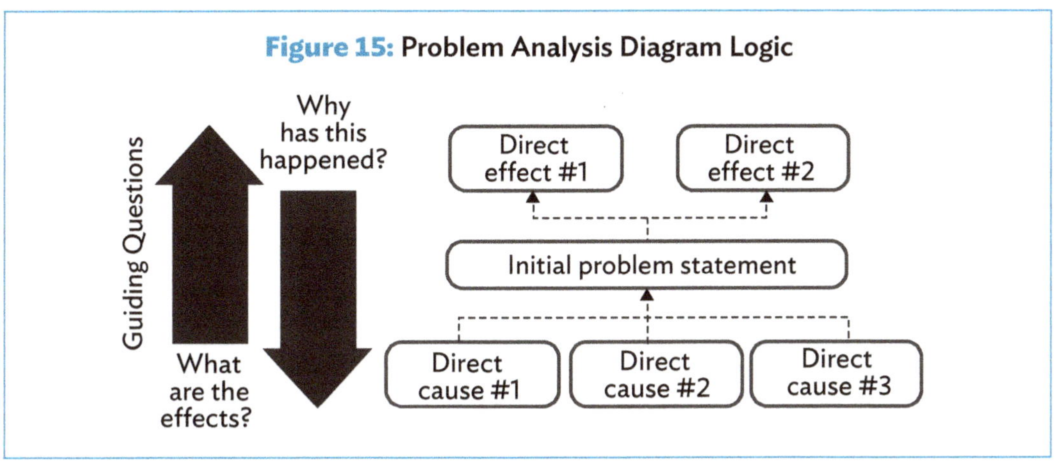

Figure 15: Problem Analysis Diagram Logic

D. Solution Development and Results Analysis

The findings of a thorough situation analysis are the foundation from which the project team can develop the right solutions to achieve the desired development results. Moving from situation analysis to solution development involves identifying and analyzing desired results and scoping a package of effective solutions that is realistically implementable, given the resources available. Like problem analysis, these steps should be undertaken in a participatory manner, in consultation with key stakeholders identified during the stakeholder analysis. The ToC is a useful analytical approach for undertaking solution development and results analysis, which are two iterative processes that inform each other.

Theory of change approach. Every project design has an underlying ToC, which is essentially a set of expectations held by the project team about how the project will bring about positive change for its intended beneficiaries. A good project design is based on a well-researched (i.e., evidence-based) ToC, developed in consultation with, and agreed upon by, key stakeholders. Applying the ToC approach involves making the ToC explicit and using it as a tool to help develop and communicate a fitting project design, and support project management and evaluation.

Making the ToC explicit involves specifying the project's development hypothesis by mapping the pathways of change between the results the project aims to achieve (outputs and outcome), how the project plans to achieve them (activities), and the assumptions and risks underlying these change pathways. Although the results chain as depicted in the DMF shows a linear logical chain leading to the outcome, the cause-and-effect relationships are rarely simple and linear. Mapping out the ToC helps the project design team comprehensively think through the complexity of the change process and can stimulate innovative project designs. The ToC is best mapped and communicated with a diagram and accompanying narrative. Figure 16 provides an illustrative example of a ToC diagram template.

Applying the theory of change approach to ADB projects. At the very least, the project description narrative in the RRP should outline the basic ToC of the project by explaining the essential cause-and-effect relationships between the project's outputs and outcome, identifying critical assumptions and risks, and justifying these and other project design choices with evidence from a robust economic, and poverty and social analyses;[12] evidence and lessons from other comparable interventions (including by other development partners, government, and civil society); and evaluations or other research.

---

[12] A project's results logic should be founded on robust economic, and poverty and social analyses. The economic analysis tests and establishes the economic rationale and viability of the proposed design, including an analysis of alternative designs or projects. The poverty and social analysis assesses the key poverty and social issues of the potential beneficiaries, including the project's impact channels and expected systemic changes. Refer to ADB. 2017. *Guidelines for the Economic Analysis of Projects*; ADB. 2023. Bank Policy on Incorporation of Social Dimensions into ADB Operations. *Operations Manual.* OM Section C3; ADB. 2023. Bank Policy on Economic Analysis of Projects. *Operations Manual.* OM Section G1; and ADB. 2024. *Environment and Social Framework.*

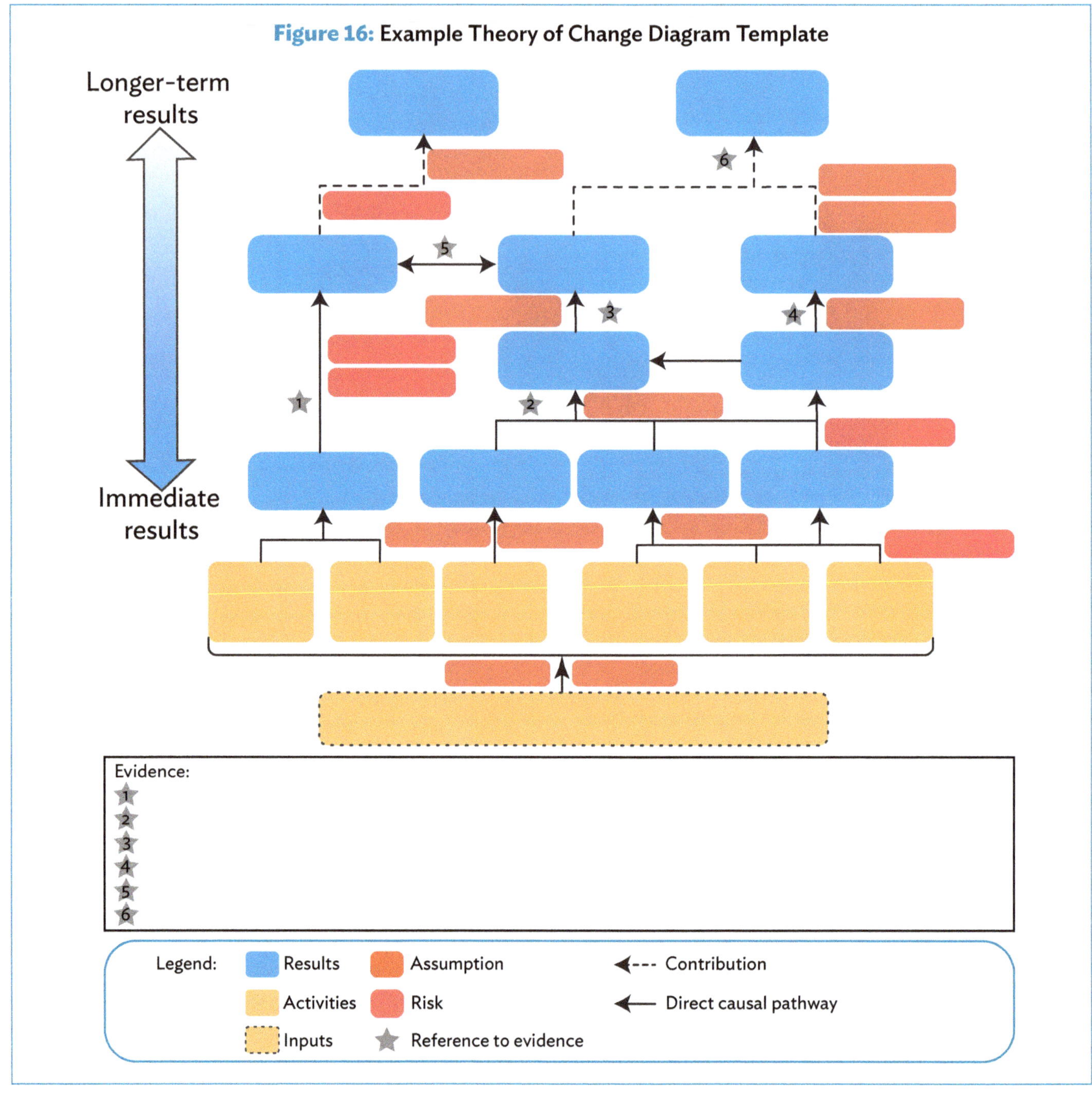

Figure 16: Example Theory of Change Diagram Template

Project teams may also decide to prepare a more comprehensive ToC analysis and visualize it in a ToC diagram (Box 17). While the ToC can be described in narrative form, visualizing it in a flowchart yields a helpful analytical and communication tool. A flowchart is especially useful for complex, multi-issue, or multisector project designs because it helps the design team identify and comprehensively think through the multifaceted change pathways. It is also an effective visual means for communicating the ToC to key project stakeholders, including reviewers and project managers.

When DMCs approach ADB to finance a project that they have already identified, and may also have designed to some degree, it can still be useful to map out the ToC to ensure the design is relevant and comprehensive enough to sustainably solve the targeted development problems, and to confirm the design with key stakeholders. In cases where ADB replicates a common or previously implemented project design in a new location, mapping out the ToC can help ensure the design suits the contextual particularities of the new location.

Box 17: Tips for Visualizing and Communicating the Theory of Change

(i)   The theory of change (ToC) can be mapped in differing forms and formats and contain varying depths of information and detail. A vertical flowchart diagram design is recommended as it mirrors the vertical logic of the design and monitoring framework.

(ii) No matter what style is selected, a good ToC mapping should be logical, show detailed coherent cause-and-effect pathways, and clearly communicate how the project design is expected to achieve the intended results.

(iii) It is challenging to capture all the key details in a ToC diagram. Include a supporting narrative that explains the details and includes the evidence basis underpinning the cause-and-effect pathways.

Process. Mapping the ToC is an iterative process. Start simple and build it out over the course of project preparation. Mapping the ToC collaboratively with key stakeholders helps develop effective solutions and a shared understanding among stakeholders of what the project will try to accomplish and how. It is also useful to build consensus on how success will be measured and documented. While the process is ideally undertaken collaboratively with key stakeholders in a series of workshops, alternative approaches can be adopted to suit the operational realities of different project contexts (Box 18).

Suggested steps for undertaking solution development and results analysis using the ToC approach are as follows:

(i)   **Identify starter result(s).** Considering the findings from the problem analysis, convert the problem statements into result statements—positive statements that describe the situation after the problems have been resolved, or the change we want to achieve, e.g., "youth perceive secondary school as irrelevant" may become "secondary school curriculum is engaging and relevant to labor market demands."

(a) Ensure result statements are phrased as specifically as possible, including identifying who or what should have changed in what way and specifying the intended beneficiaries; the statements should also be ambitious yet realistic for a project to deliver. For example, the problem statement "cost of transporting goods to market is prohibitive for farmers" may become a result statement such as "cost of transporting goods to market is more affordable for farmers," not "transport of goods to market is free of cost."

(b) The problem analysis diagram can be converted into a skeleton of the ToC simply by converting all problem statements into result statements.

Box 18: Tips for Applying Good Practices to Suit Operational Realities— Mapping the Theory of Change

There is no substitute for a highly participatory approach to mapping the theory of change (ToC), but it is not always feasible. Operational realities sometimes require alternative approaches to be taken. Common challenges include tight project preparation timelines and the impracticality of gathering all key stakeholders. In these cases, the following are alternative approaches that can be taken (in order, from more to less ideal):

(i)   The Asian Development Bank (ADB) project team drafts the ToC and performance indicators via a participatory in-person or virtual workshop with key stakeholders. The ADB team subsequently finalizes the ToC and prepares a draft design and monitoring framework (DMF), which it then shares with key project stakeholders for feedback and input.

(ii) The ADB project team drafts the ToC and performance indicators for the project and shares and finalizes them with key stakeholders via participatory workshops.

(iii) The ADB project team drafts the ToC and DMF for the project and shares it electronically with key project stakeholders for feedback and input.

In cases where a project DMF has already been developed, mapping the ToC underlying it can still be a helpful tool for validating the project results chain and design, and identifying any needed adjustments. Regardless of the approach taken, it is essential to allocate time with key stakeholders to review and discuss the ToC and DMF at the project launch.

(ii) **Map the pathways of change.** Starting from the highest-level result statements, work backward step-by-step to identify what needs to change before the situation described in the level above can be achieved or occurs. This process is called "backward mapping" because it involves starting at the higher-level results and working backward to the beginning by repeatedly asking, "What are the necessary preconditions for the above change to occur?"

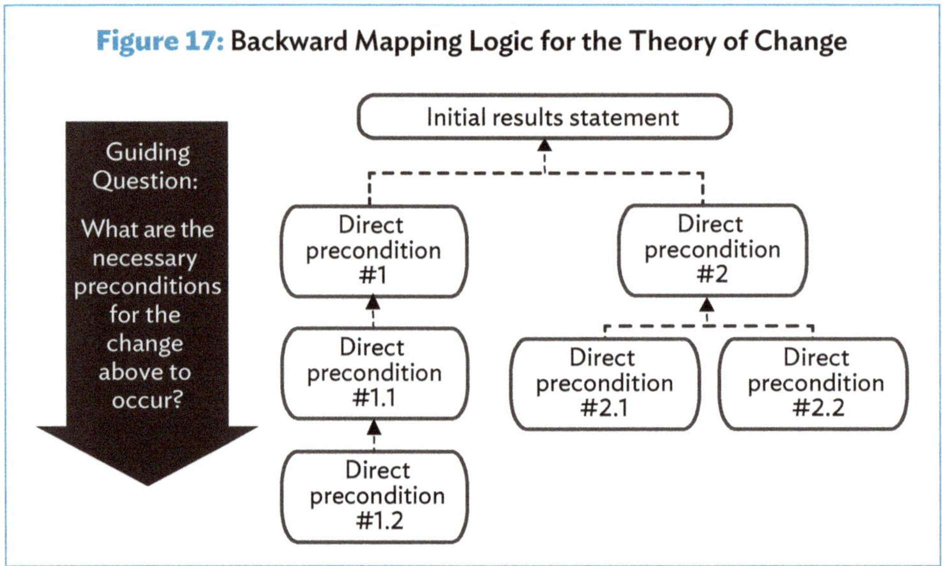

Figure 17: Backward Mapping Logic for the Theory of Change

Figure 17 illustrates the question-and-answer logic used to build the diagram. Review and refine the cause-and-effect pathways ensuring there are no leaps in logic between statements.

(a) In each result statement, make sure to name the stakeholders involved and their changed behavior, performance, or situation. At each level, answer and specify, "Who is doing what differently?" and "What is there that was not there before?"

(b) Tip: Often, project design teams are inclined to focus on what they or the project must do to create the desired change. This trap of jumping to project activities should be avoided because it prematurely narrows creativity in project design down to the familiar menu of activities. There is a simple way to help avoid the activities-focused trap: the result statements must be "change" statements. They should not say anything about what the project is doing. For example, avoid a statement like "train staff in organization X;" instead use "staff of organization X have improved knowledge of Y topic." This approach spurs innovation by encouraging teams to brainstorm various strategies for bringing about the desired changes.

Box 19 provides some tips on tools and applications that can be used to map a ToC.

(iii) **Identify change pathway owners and explore solutions and project design strategies.** Develop appropriate solutions that can achieve the desired results.

(a) Identify which stakeholders have the most influence on, and vested interest in, achieving changes in each pathway of change. They may be the holders of the official mandate for improving undesirable conditions; stakeholder groups that need to coordinate their regular tasks and resources to achieve a change; or individuals who wield official or unofficial power to champion or lead a change process. This information should be available from the stakeholder analysis.

(b) Identify project design strategies (sets of outputs and activities) that can bring about or influence the desired changes. Based on the list of options, consult with the main owners of the change pathways to identify outputs and activities that are the most relevant, promising, and feasible.

(c) If not already mapped, add these outputs and activities to the ToC diagram.

Box 19: Tips on Tools for Mapping the Theory of Change

Various tools and applications can be used to build a theory of change diagram in a participatory manner. A common approach is to convene the key stakeholders (physically or virtually) and use sticky notes to brainstorm. Sticky notes can be moved and reordered making this a helpful and accessible way to engage participants. In this approach, participants work together to draft result statements (one per sticky note) and then organize them in a flowchart. Various software and web-based applications support a versatile mock-up of flowcharts and virtual team cocreating.

(iv) **Articulate assumptions and risks.** Note the assumptions and risks inherent in your pathways of change, especially with respect to the following:

   (a) The causal relationship between activities and outputs, and outputs and outcomes in the pathway. Ask: "If X changes, will Z really happen? Why? Under which conditions would this work? What might derail this? Is there anything we are taking for granted?"

   (b) The response of stakeholders to specific project activities and outputs and the changes that are expected as a result. Ask: "Are our assumptions about causality valid for all stakeholder groups and subgroups (e.g., women and men, the poor people and marginalized groups)? Will some stakeholder groups respond or behave differently than others?"

   (c) (Pre)conditions in the project context that need to be in place for the desired change to occur. Ask: "What evidence do we have that supports our assumptions about causality and the effectiveness of the selected project design? What risks could derail our plan?"

   (d) See **Section II.D** for further guidance on identifying and analyzing assumptions and risks and the decision tree for identifying critical assumptions in **Figure 10**.

   The analysis of assumptions and risks may reveal that adjustments to the change pathways are required, and/or that additional outputs or activities will be needed to bring about the desired changes for all intended beneficiaries.

(v) **Consider unintended effects and sustainability.** Review the ToC asking the following questions:

   (a) "Are there any unintended consequences—positive or negative—that may occur as a consequence of planned activities or the achievement of intended results?" Note these and adjust project design and/or identify risks to be mitigated, as necessary.

   (b) "Will the intended results be sustained beyond project completion? Which beneficiaries' needs will continue during the post-completion phase?" Adjust project design as necessary to include the inputs and activities required to sustain the results. Identify the risks to achieving sustainability readiness and possible mitigating measures.

(vi) **Confirm project scope.** A fully developed ToC diagram will contain a series of results chains (outputs and outcomes). Confirm which results chains the project will deliver. Each stakeholder group, the executing agency, and the project team need to clearly understand how moving forward with a particular results chain will affect them directly or indirectly.

   (a) During this analysis, consider the available resources, capacities of the executing and implementing agencies, interests of the intended beneficiaries, political feasibility, and other variables affecting successful implementation of the results chain. If a results chain owner is unable to commit to its achievement, consider whether the strategy for achieving the results chain should be improved so the results chain owner stands a better chance of success. Solutions may come from expert knowledge, best practices, and lessons from other projects or programs. If the results chain owner accepts this new strategy, then include this results chain branch in the project's scope. If the results chain owner cannot accept the strategy, these results chains must be excluded from the project.

   (b) Identify which clusters of outputs will be delivered by the ADB-financed project. In so doing, confirm their suitability given ADB project selection criteria. These may be economic, financial, socioeconomic, environmental, technical, and/or institutional, including ADB's safeguard and other applicable ADB policies. If other outputs are "owned" by other stakeholders, then identify those as well.

(vii) **Review and refine the theory of change.** Revise the ToC based on the confirmed project scope. This may involve removing some results chains and revising others.

  (a) Review the ToC from the bottom up, asking: "Is this change or condition sufficient for the next one to happen? If not, what is missing?" Add it. "Is this change or condition necessary for the next one to happen?" If not, remove it.

  (b) Ensure cause-and-effect pathways are supported by evidence, including from the project's economic, and poverty and social analyses, as appropriate. Flag the pathways where further evidence and information are needed and make plans to collect these during project preparation.

  (c) Review assumptions and risks and reconsider unintended consequences and sustainability factors.

(viii) **Finalize project.** Carry out feasibility studies and any other necessary analyses for project preparation. Based on the findings, decide on the most appropriate strategies and results to be pursued under the proposed project. The collective involvement of the borrower, executing agency, other key stakeholders (as appropriate), and ADB is critical at this stage. The final decision should be based on consensus to ensure ownership of the project and to maximize the probability of achieving the desired results. Other issues to keep in mind when finalizing the project include the following:

  (a) Does it conform to local laws, policies, and procedures?

  (b) Are the requisite expertise and capacity available to carry it out?

  (c) Is it affordable and cost effective, and is the necessary financing available?

  (d) Is it socially acceptable to the target beneficiaries?

  (e) Is it likely to result in any negative externalities that will require mitigation?

  (f) Is it supported by other investments and projects that are ongoing or planned by the government, ADB, or other organizations?

  (g) What are the major risks and how can they be mitigated? Are critical assumptions expected to hold true?

Once the ToC is mapped, the project team will be well-positioned to formulate a good DMF and prepare a relevant detailed project design. The ToC mapping (diagram and narrative) is a working document that can be updated to reflect learning and changes in context over the course of the project cycle.

E. Formulate the Content of the Design and Monitoring Framework

Once the results analysis is finished, the DMF template can be completed by taking the following steps (refer to **Section II** of these guidelines for detailed guidance on each part of the DMF):

(i) **Develop outcome statement.** Referring to the characteristics of an outcome defined in **Box 2**, develop the DMF outcome statement. Only one outcome statement should be developed for each project. Ensure it captures the planned change. Working from the ToC diagram, the outcome statement can be developed by selecting an appropriate solution statement from the diagram or combining several outcome-level solution statements.

(ii) **Clarify impact statements.** Clarify between one and three impact statements the project will be aligned with. Each statement should ideally be sourced from the ADB CPS, or national development or sector strategies or plans.

(iii) **Decide on output statements.** Decide which outputs are necessary and sufficient to achieve the project outcome. Review the DMF results chain logic. Check that there is a strong cause-and-effect relationship between the outputs and outcome.

(iv) **Include critical assumptions and risks.** Add critical assumptions, including assumptions for partner financing, and risks for the two levels of the results chain (activities to outputs and outputs to outcome). Assumptions and risks fill in the cause-and-effect gaps between results levels. Working from the ToC diagram, simply transfer the critical assumption and risk statements into the risk assessment and risk management plan (RAMP) and DMF following the guidance in **Section II.D**. In addition, any solution statements in the ToC that sit between the selected DMF outcome and outputs statements can be converted into assumptions or risks and transferred into the DMF as appropriate. Review the results chain logic as completing the risks and critical assumptions column may lead to changes in the DMF results chain.

(v) **Develop performance indicators and set targets.** Include at least one performance indicator for each outcome and output statement. The ToC diagram is a helpful tool for developing performance indicators. Solution statements in the ToC that sit between the selected DMF outcome and output statements can inform performance indicators, in particular leading indicators of the DMF outcome. Identify targets for each indicator. Ensure outcome-level targets are consistent with the economic and financial analysis (Box 20) and realistically achievable within the first full year of operation following physical completion, or before financial closure of project. Review the results chain and ensure that the performance indicators measure all dimensions of the corresponding result statement. The selection of performance indicators may lead to reconsideration of the DMF results chain, particularly the outcome statement.

(vi) **List data sources and reporting mechanisms.** For each performance indicator, list the data collection methods to be used for primary data collection and the data sources and reporting mechanisms for secondary data.

(vii) **Determine activities.** Determine the key activities necessary to produce the outputs. Do this sequentially for each output. Agree on milestones for each activity and include them in brackets after each activity description. It is also good practice to list key project management activities at the end of the activities row.

(viii) **Review results chain logic.** Consideration of the activities may lead to adjustment of the outputs. In this case, reexamine the full results chain as it may need final adjustment.

(ix) **List inputs.** List the inputs required to carry out the activities by source (e.g., ADB, government, and beneficiaries).

(x) **Specify alignment with Strategy 2030 development results.** Review the DMF performance indicators and tag them to each development results indicator for which the project is expected to contribute results. In case a project is expected to contribute results to a development results indicator yet the link to any of the DMF indicators is absent, the fact of alignment should be entered in ADB's portfolio management system.

Box 20: Consistency with Economic and Financial Analysis

The economic and financial viability of the project and the sustainability of its benefits are assessed at the appraisal stage. The assessment is based on the project structure, usually captured in an early draft of the design and monitoring framework (DMF), which identifies, quantifies, and enables the valuation of sustained benefits throughout the working life of the investment. The DMF outcome statement and the performance indicators and their target values should be aligned with the economic and financial analysis. The target amounts and dates should match the annual benefit stream used in the economic analysis. For example, in an urban rail project, the economic analysis may in part be based on the average daily number of passengers in each year of operation. The benefit stream will include many years of operation in line with the working life of the urban rail system. The DMF outcome indicator could have a target date of the first full year of operation. The target value of the "average daily number of passengers in the first full year of operation" should be the same in the DMF and the economic analysis. There must be consistency between the DMF and the economic analysis for all output and outcome benefits articulated in results statements, indicators, and targets.

IV. USING THE DESIGN AND MONITORING FRAMEWORK DURING IMPLEMENTATION AND AT COMPLETION

A. Results Monitoring and Evaluation Arrangements

Results monitoring and evaluation (M&E) are integral to managing for development results and good project management generally. Information produced through these processes is essential to those managing and overseeing project implementation. It is also used to meet reporting accountabilities to a variety of stakeholders (including ADB, DMCs, investors, development partners, and civil society) about progress and performance, and is a means to support organizational learning and continuous improvement.

M&E are two complementary but distinct processes (Table 5).

In addition to a good DMF, a strong M&E plan consists of four key elements: clear activity planning, clear designation of roles, quality assurance, and budget (Box 21). The M&E plan for sovereign operations is outlined in the project administration manual (PAM).

Results monitoring responsibilities. The borrower, typically through its implementing agency, is responsible for collecting results data, and reporting and using the information for monitoring purposes during implementation.[13] In addition to its own monitoring activities, the ADB project team relies on the borrower's reports to monitor progress and inform management. Therefore, ADB must ensure that adequate results monitoring arrangements are in place. Results monitoring arrangements proposed during project preparation need to reflect the borrower's institutional capacity and address any issues related to staffing, processes, accountabilities and responsibilities, knowledge, skills, equipment, and budget required to carry out this monitoring function. As part of

its design, a project can include an explicit component for improving the borrower's results monitoring capacity, or ADB can support this via a wider institutional capacity development initiative. Production of statistical information is essential, but it is equally important to develop the capacity to use this data in planning and decision-making. Larger projects may need an M&E specialist on the project implementation team.

Planning for self-evaluations. This guidance focuses specifically on self-evaluation (refer to Table 5 for the distinction between self- and independent evaluation). During the project design phase, project teams should prepare for planned and potential self-evaluations by ensuring that they are adequately budgeted for and that the baseline data and any additional information that may be required will be available to evaluators at the appropriate time.

(i) **When to conduct additional self-evaluations.** In addition to the mandatory self-evaluations (project completion report [PCR] and TA completion report), it may be worthwhile conducting more in-depth self-evaluations to help better understand what is working well for the project, what is not and why, and gain insights about how to improve current and future projects. This may take the form of a midterm self-evaluation or an impact evaluation study.

(a) A **midterm self-evaluation** can help the project team identify and understand issues in design, implementation, and management, and devise appropriate actions to address them. This is a deeper investigation into project performance and questions of interest to project management than that undertaken during a standard ADB midterm review and can be particularly useful for complex and problem projects.

---

[13] ADB. 2011. Bank Policy on Project Performance Management System. *Operations Manual.* OM Section J1/BP.

Table 5: Project Results Monitoring and Evaluation at ADB: What, When, and by Whom?

Item	Project Results Monitoring	Project Evaluation	
What?	Tracking inputs, activities, outputs, outcomes, and other aspects of the project	Assessment of the extent of results achievement and implementation performance along some key dimensions	
	Focuses mainly on delivery of activities and outputs; monitoring risks, assumptions, and for unintended effects; and, most importantly, tracking progress toward the intended outcome	Focuses on both expected and achieved outcome, examining results chains, implementation processes, contextual factors, and causality	
Why?	To ensure successful project implementation	To understand the range of factors that contribute to or constrain the achievement of results, to learn, and for accountability	
When?	Continuously throughout project implementation as an integral part of project management and supervision	At specific points during project implementation (e.g., a midterm evaluation), at completion, and/or post-completion	
By Whom?	Implementing and executing agencies in developing member countries, ADB project administration team, and sometimes by an independent monitor (e.g., for results-based lending)	Self-evaluation	Independent evaluation
		A unit or individuals reporting to the management of the funder, partner, or implementing organization; e.g., implementing and executing agencies in developing member countries, ADB project administration team, or consultants hired by these	Entities and individuals free from the control of those responsible for the design and implementation of the project, such as ADB's Independent Evaluation Department

ADB = Asian Development Bank.

Box 21: Key Elements of a Strong Monitoring and Evaluation Plan

(i) **Clear activity planning (including timelines) for data collection, analysis, and reporting.** Information produced should be relevant and timely and should respond to the needs of different users (e.g., project management, developing member countries, the Asian Development Bank, and intended project beneficiaries).

(ii) **Clear designation of roles and responsibilities.** Key stakeholders should be actively involved in planning, collecting, reviewing, and interpreting performance information to the extent possible. Project monitoring arrangements should be integrated into the developing member country's existing management systems. Roles and responsibilities should be clearly outlined in the consultants' terms of reference.

(iii) **Quality assurance plans.** Capacity should be in place for collecting, analyzing, verifying, and reporting timely and valid performance information.

(iv) **Budget allocations covering anticipated costs.** Requisite monitoring and evaluation costs should be budgeted for in the project management and administration budget line and detailed in the project administration manual.

(b) It may be worth investing in an **impact evaluation study** to understand more rigorously what works and how by measuring which changes are attributable to a project, especially for innovative project designs that do not have a record of success yet and for designs being considered for expansion or replication. Impact evaluation methods are often needed to test whether critical assumptions in the project's ToC held true in practice and identify unintended effects.[14]

(ii) **Budgeting for self-evaluation.** Budgets vary based on the self-evaluation's scale and location, the cost of experts, and the level of complexity of the methodologies and data collection tools required to answer the chosen evaluation questions. These costs will vary based on local capacity and availability of data. An under-resourced self-evaluation risks being a suboptimal investment. ADB has TA funds to resource impact evaluations. TA funds can be used to fund self-evaluation activities conducted during the project design phase (e.g., evaluation design planning and baseline studies). It is advisable to include the

---

[14] For detailed guidance see ADB. 2017. *Impact Evaluation of Development Interventions: A Practical Guide.*

necessary consultants (e.g., PCR consultants and survey specialists) in the project implementation budget. The PAM should detail the budget and other key information about the required self-evaluations and any additional self-evaluations ADB and the DMC agree to conduct, including draft consultant terms of reference.

There are numerous research tools and methods for collecting information to support project monitoring and enrich self-evaluations (Box 10).[15] ADB staff are also able to provide guidance on designing and funding impact evaluations, and on evaluation designs and methodologies.

B. Implementation

The DMF is a core element of ADB's project performance management system. Regularly collecting data on the project's performance indicators throughout the implementation period provides managers and stakeholders with up-to-date information on progress toward the desired outcome. This enables managers to identify strengths and problems as they occur so that they can take corrective action in a timely manner to best ensure the intended outcome is achieved.

ADB's supervision role involves providing technical guidance and operational supervision to projects under implementation. ADB staff monitor the projects based on their DMFs by reviewing reports, conducting site visits, cross-referencing with other stakeholders, or sometimes by hiring external monitors. Candid and timely monitoring of a project's DMF is essential to alert the borrower, cofinanciers, managers, and concerned ADB staff about any issues that may arise during implementation and take any proactive measures needed, such as project restructuring, to enhance the likelihood of the project meeting its objectives.

Incorporating monitoring and evaluation into project launch activities. After project approval and signing of the legal agreements, the ADB project team works with the borrower to ensure that the required M&E systems are in place. During the project inception mission, the ADB project team should meet with executing and implementing agency staff and other key stakeholders to review and discuss the DMF, bearing in mind that there are likely to be new staff in the project implementation unit and other

new key stakeholders who were not involved in designing the project. It is important to ensure all key stakeholders clearly understand and agree on the project's objectives and how success will be measured. The ADB project team should also discuss the details of the M&E plan in the PAM with the stakeholders and agree on any necessary revisions or additions. In these discussions, it is helpful for the project team to (i) explain and confirm monitoring and reporting requirements, including report formats and timelines; (ii) confirm data collection methodologies and sources, as these may need to be updated or further specified; and (iii) ensure M&E systems and resources are in place, including clear assignment of responsibility for data collection and reporting. If adequate systems are not in place, a clear plan should be developed to establish them (footnote 11).

Using the design and monitoring framework for project monitoring. The DMF provides results-focused structure for project monitoring. ADB review missions, including the in-depth midterm review, assess whether the project's outputs are being delivered or if adjustments are required to ensure that the outcome is likely to be achieved. The borrower's progress reports should provide the same analysis. Where necessary, remedial measures with an action plan are agreed between ADB and the borrower (Box 22).

Box 22: Tips for Using the Design and Monitoring Framework as a Project Management and Supervision Tool

Effectively using the design and monitoring framework as a project management and supervision tool entails

(i) regularly monitoring and reporting on progress against indicator targets;

(ii) explaining and discussing variance (actual performance vs. targets);

(iii) identifying problems by flagging issues and risks, and creating and assigning an action plan to address them; and

(iv) reviewing the design and monitoring framework and adjusting it when needed to reflect changing circumstances and project environments.

Source: ADB. 2011. Bank Policy on Project Performance Management System. *Operations Manual.* OM Section J1/BP.

---

[15] For an overview of tools and data collection methods for poverty and social analysis and their application to ADB-financed operations consult Appendix II of ADB. 2012. *Handbook on Poverty and Social Analysis: A Working Document.*

Any adjustments to outputs, output indicators, activities, and risks and critical assumptions as well as further specification of the outcome and outcome indicators are attached to the back-to-office report of the review mission, reflected in a revised DMF, and transferred to a performance report.

Changing the design and monitoring framework after project approval. Adjusting the DMF is critical to ensure it remains a relevant monitoring and evaluation tool. The DMF should be adjusted when needed to reflect changing circumstances and project environments so that the intended project outcome can be achieved (footnote 13). Any revisions to the DMF should be agreed to by ADB and the borrower. The revised DMF clearly identifies which content in the latest approved DMF has been added, deleted, or amended.

The DMF can be revised at any point during project implementation (**Box 23**). Changes should be made as soon as the need becomes apparent and ideally during the early stages of implementation. A project's midpoint is also an opportune time. By bringing together an experienced and complementary team of mission members, the midterm review mission is well placed to conduct an in-depth assessment with the borrower of whether the project is likely to achieve its outcome and outputs on time and within budget, and to consider whether the outcome and output targets remain relevant in the current project context and environment. It is often helpful to hire an M&E consultant to support the midterm review.

Box 23: When to Change the Design and Monitoring Framework

When considering whether to change the design and monitoring framework (DMF), project teams must respect the DMF's dual purpose as a tool for project management and for accountability. When performance is falling behind target, remedial actions should be taken to put the project back on track. The DMF should not be changed solely to revise targets because the project risks not achieving them. DMF changes should reflect adjustments in project design undertaken to respond to a change in the project context or environment to maximize the development results achieved.

Additional financing. Additional financing requires a revised DMF as part of the approval documentation. The RRP for additional financing restates the project's results and indicators and clarifies whether they have changed on account of the additional financing. It is expected that a request to add significant additional financing to scale up and/or restructure an ongoing project will entail changes to the outputs and/or outcomes of the project's DMF. The RRP for additional financing contains a revised DMF that compares the ongoing project (before additional financing) with the project with additional financing.

C. Completion

Project completion. The main objectives of a completion report are to evaluate performance to enhance transparency and accountability and to learn from operational experience to improve the design and implementation of ongoing and future projects. The completion report for sovereign operations presents the self-evaluation of overall project performance and rates the project's success based on an assessment using the core criteria of relevance, effectiveness, efficiency, and sustainability. This is complemented by an assessment using the non-core criteria of development impacts, ADB and cofinancier performance, and borrower and executing agency performance. For TA, the completion report assesses the development results and rates TA performance using the core criteria of relevance, effectiveness, and efficiency. This is complemented by an assessment of the likelihood that the TA results will be sustained.

The DMF serves as the basis for the completion report prepared by ADB and the borrower. It informs the assessment on most of the evaluation criteria, but especially the project's effectiveness rating, which is based on an assessment of the achievement of the outputs and outcome based on targets in the DMF, including any revisions approved during implementation (footnote 13). Thus, the most recently approved DMF forms the basis for preparing the completion report and subsequent independent evaluations, such as project performance evaluation reports, and the original DMF is referenced if relevant.[16]

---

[16]   ADB. 2016. *Guidelines for the Evaluation of Public Sector Operations.*

The PCR for sovereign investment projects should be circulated within 12 months after the financial closing date of the project. The completion report for TA should be circulated within 6 months of its financial closing date.[17] Outcome-level indicators and targets in the DMF should be set considering these circulation timelines to ensure outcome data are available to include in the completion report.

For detailed guidance on preparing a PCR, consult ADB's *Guidelines for the Evaluation of Public Sector Operations* (footnote 16). For guidance on preparing a TA completion report, consult ADB's *Technical Assistance Completion Report Validation Guidelines.*[18]

---

[17] Procedures for various modalities and financing, in particular for policy-based lending and the multitranche financing facility, differ and are outlined in Project Administration Instructions 6.06 (ADB. 2024. Project Completion Report for Sovereign Operations. *Project Administration Instructions.* PAI 6.06).

[18] ADB. 2020. *Technical Assistance Completion Report Validation Guidelines.*